The Portfolio

THIRD EDITION

Connection

This book is dedicated to the teachers who make a difference
in the lives of children every day. They inspire us and lead us to a better future.

The Portfolio Connection

THIRD EDITION

Connection

STUDENT WORK LINKED TO STANDARDS

Susan **BELGRAD** • Kay **BURKE** • Robin **FOGARTY**

CORWIN PRESS
A SAGE Company
Thousand Oaks, CA 91320

For information:

Corwin Press
A SAGE Company
2455 Teller Road
Thousand Oaks, California 91320
www.corwinpress.com

SAGE Ltd.
1 Oliver's Yard
55 City Road
London EC1Y 1SP
United Kingdom

SAGE Pvt. Ltd.
B 1/I 1 Mohan Cooperative
   Industrial Area
Mathura Road, New Delhi 110 044
India

SAGE Asia-Pacific Pte. Ltd.
33 Pekin Street #02–01
Far East Square
Singapore 048763

Printed in the United States of America

Library of Congress Cataloging-in-Publication Data

Belgrad, Susan.
The portfolio connection: student work linked to standards/by Susan Belgrad, Kay Burke & Robin Fogarty. — 3rd ed.
      p. cm.
Prev. ed. entered under Kay Burke.
Includes bibliographical references and index.
ISBN 978-1-4129-5973-5 (cloth: acid-free paper)
ISBN 978-1-4129-5974-2 (pbk.: acid-free paper)
   1. Portfolios in education. 2. Educational tests and measurements. I. Burke, Kay. II. Fogarty, Robin. III. Burke, Kay. Portfolio connection. IV. Title.

LB1029.P67B87 2008
371.26′4—dc22   2007046627

This book is printed on acid-free paper.

08   09   10   11   12   10 9 8 7 6 5 4 3 2 1

Acquisitions Editor:	Hudson Perigo
Editorial Assistants:	Lesley Blake, Cassandra Harris
Production Editor:	Veronica Stapleton
Copy Editor:	Alison Hope
Typesetter:	C&M Digitals (P) Ltd.
Proofreader:	Caryne Brown
Indexer:	Sheila Bodell
Cover Designer:	Rose Storey
Graphic Designer:	Scott Van Atta

Contents

Preface

The first edition of *The Portfolio Connection* was envisioned as "just a little book" by the authors in 1993. At that time, portfolios had just arrived on the horizon of authentic assessment. It was natural for us to think metaphorically about academic portfolios as the artists' showcase of their accomplished and evolving media. The chapter titles flowed effortlessly into many of the images of an artist selecting the work that best "spoke" or gave voice to his or her body of work. The artist-centered actions of *projecting* the purposes of the portfolio, then *interjecting* individuality, *self-assessing* the product using the relevant standard, and *perfecting* the message of the work became the inspiration that led our thinking and conversation throughout the book's chapters.

The trend toward authentic assessment of student learning was well under way in 1993. There was a great deal of hope that alignment between a student-centered curriculum and instruction, together with collections of evidence of student performance, might forestall the achievement-testing tidal wave that was about to sweep across the United States. The book anticipated that educators would need to have clear purposes and comprehensible procedures for students to collect work samples over time, store them efficiently, and ultimately select them as the messages about themselves that they believed would "tell their story of learning and achievement."

While seven of the chapters addressed the portfolio process, the final two chapters briefly touched the top of the rich canopy of portfolio assessment—the presentation. Since the first and second editions of *The Portfolio Connection* were published, it has become clear that student voice must be positioned at the center of the portfolio process. Similarly, the audience, or "gallery" where that voice is heard, is in essence the true goal of portfolios and electronic portfolios (e-portfolios)—to assess, evaluate, respect, and celebrate accomplishments.

The second edition of *The Portfolio Connection* was published in 2002. While its content was not substantially changed, it addressed the arrival of electronic media as an important new "container" for the academic portfolio. The e-portfolio, complete with multimedia, including audio and video evidence and student reflection, has since transformed the landscape of authentic assessment. Advances and availability of technology have brought many more opportunities for educators and the students they teach to "tell the story" of their lives as learners—and as readers, writers, social scientists, mathematical and scientific thinkers, and, yes, artists.

This edition of *The Portfolio Connection* returns to the metaphor of the artist with its focus on the student at the center of the learning and assessment process. It further develops the image of the artist's metacognition and voice as the artist sets standards for the work, and applies this image to the student portfolio process. It looks at the critical inquiry and creativity that the artist surely uses in determining if each piece truly speaks for the essence of his or her ability and talent. It envisions the K–12 student engaged in the very same reflection. It also aligns the portfolio process with the evolving authentic assessment movement. Rather than assessment *of* student learning, the portfolio is now positioned as representing assessment *for* student learning. It explores the innovation promised by the e-portfolio and provides a number of ideas, resources, and procedures for safely sailing the elementary and secondary student into cyberspace.

WHAT'S NEW IN THIS EDITION?

- Addition of e-portfolios throughout the book
- More attention to international perspectives on portfolios
- More examples, samples, and blacklines (tools that are needed, useful, and well executed) in all chapters
- More portfolio examples for different grade levels, and for children with special needs
- Expanded ideas of how portfolios become integrated within curricula and student voice
- More information on portfolio conferences and Web showcases
- More information on how and when to get parents involved
- Discussion of the impact of the No Child Left Behind Act on student assessment
- Additional information on student peer assessment

Acknowledgments

Heartfelt gratitude for persistence and commitment to the timely production of this book is extended to Hudson Perigo, Executive Editor; Veronica Stapleton, Production Editor; and Editorial Assistants Lesley Blake and Cassandra Harris. Many thanks go to Alison Hope for her editorial assistance that enhanced the quality and readability throughout the book. We gratefully acknowledge the work of professional educators in the United States, Canada, Australia, and the United Kingdom who have made important contributions reflected in this book that promote student voice and achievement in classrooms everywhere.

Corwin Press thanks the following individuals for their contributions to this work:

Alice M. Atkinson
Associate Professor Emeritus
Iowa City, IA

Michael F. Dwyer
English Department Chair
Otter Valley Union High School
Brandon, VT

Stephanie Jones
Teacher
Forrest City High School
Forrest City, AR

About the Authors

 **Susan Belgrad**, PhD, has taught in elementary and early childhood special education, and has a long career in higher education working with teachers from prekindergarten through high school. Dr. Belgrad received her doctorate in Educational Administration from George Peabody College of Vanderbilt University. For the past 20 years, she has led state and national efforts that support teachers' professional education and public awareness of teacher excellence. She has trained faculty in promoting the learner-centered classroom through authentic assessment, cooperative learning, and portfolio assessment. Dr. Belgrad teaches courses in reflective practice, graduate research, curriculum development, and technology-supported learning. Her articles have been published in journals such as the *Journal of Professional Development* and the *Illinois Journal of Gifted Education*. She has written book chapters and coauthored *The Portfolio Connection: Student Work Linked to Standards* (Corwin Press, 2002).

 **Kay Burke**, PhD, has a broad base of educational experience, including serving as an award-winning classroom teacher and as a school administrator, a university instructor, and an international professional developer. She works with Kay Burke & Associates, LLC (www.kayburke.com), to provide workshops to teachers and administrators in standards-based learning, performance assessment, classroom management, mentoring, and portfolio development.

For the past 18 years, Dr. Burke has presented at state and national conferences, such as the Association for Supervision and Curriculum Development, the National Staff Development Council, the National Association of Elementary School Principals, the National Association of Secondary School Principals, the National Middle School Association, and the International Reading Association, as well as at international conferences in Canada and Australia. She is the author of 10 professional development books, and coauthor of a college textbook on assessment. Some of her books published by Corwin Press include *How to Assess Authentic Learning*, 4th ed.; *What to Do With the Kid Who . . . Developing Cooperation, Self-Discipline and Responsibility in the Classroom,*

3rd ed.; *Mentoring Guidebook Level 1: Starting the Journey,* 2nd ed.; and her latest best-selling book, *From Standards to Rubrics in Six Steps: Tools for Assessing Student Learning, K–8,* which was a 2007 Finalist for the Distinguished Achievement Award for Excellence in Educational Publishing presented by the Association of Educational Publishers.

 **Robin Fogarty,** PhD, president of Robin Fogarty and Associates, Ltd., a Chicago-based, minority-owned educational publishing and consulting company, received her doctorate in curriculum and human resource development from Loyola University of Chicago. A leading proponent of the thoughtful classroom, Dr. Fogarty has trained educators throughout the world in curriculum, instruction, and assessment strategies. She has taught at all levels, from kindergarten to college; served as an administrator; and consulted with state departments and ministries of education in the United States, Puerto Rico, Russia, Canada, Australia, New Zealand, Germany, Great Britain, Singapore, Korea, and the Netherlands. Dr. Fogarty has published articles in *Educational Leadership, Phi Delta Kappan,* and the *Journal of Staff Development.* She is the author of numerous publications, including *Brain-Compatible Classrooms; Ten Things New Teachers Need; Literacy Matters; How to Integrate the Curricula; The Adult Learner; A Look at Transfer; Close the Achievement Gap; Twelve Brain Principles; Nine Best Practices;* and *Staff Developer's Guide to Professional Learning: Designing, Presenting, Facilitating and Coaching.*

Introduction

The richness of the portfolio as a valuable assessment tool in schooling has become evident to educators in the United States and throughout the world. As academic portfolios have been introduced, implemented, and modified in classrooms, they have been defined and redefined as a container of evidence about and for student achievement. Increasingly, they are viewed as a platform or scaffolding for analysis, reflection, and—most important—conversation about students' work. Few educators would dismiss the power of portfolios to produce compelling evidence of student achievement and learning dispositions. But the reality is that implementing an effective portfolio system is very complex, and can be time consuming for many, especially at the outset.

This book will address the importance of portfolios and e-portfolios in the academic life of students and teachers. It will provide the reader with an understanding of the various definitions of print and e-portfolios, and it will promote understanding of the location of portfolios at the intersection of student evaluation and assessment. Each chapter will provide a number of strategies and tools for effectively involving the stakeholders of assessment—students, parents, teachers, and administrators—and will illustrate the ways in which portfolio assessment can inform policy makers about significant student achievement. This edition of *The Portfolio Connection* will specifically focus on how the portfolio process can result in increased student voice, self-reflection, goal setting, and academic motivation. Each chapter will integrate perspectives and points for teachers to consider as they create a portfolio process that involves students and celebrates their learning accomplishments.

Academic portfolios have been defined in numerous ways. Most commonly, they are regarded as containers or "compendiums" of specifically selected student work that meets the stated purposes of the assessment process—notably, student work representing a selection of performances. Hebert (1998) describes her school's experience with portfolios as one of discovery in which students, faculty, and parents recognize that "the real contents of a portfolio are the child's thoughts and his or her reasons for selecting a particular entry. That selection process reflects the interests and metacognitive maturity of the child and the inspiration and influence offered by the teachers" (p. 583). Some educators assert that portfolios promote "evidence *and* dialogue to identify where pupils are in their learning, where they need to go and how best to get there" (Black &

William, 2004, p. 7; emphasis in original). Black and William believe that portfolios work best when they are seen as a principal means of assessing *for* learning rather than simply evaluation *of* learning. But portfolios can achieve both assessment and evaluation, as stressed by other educators. Black and William believe that educators who use portfolios provide "clear evidence about how to drive up individual attainment; clear feedback for and from pupils so there is clarity on what they need to improve and how best they can do so" (p. 8).

While portfolios and e-portfolios are considered a form of alternative assessment that includes samples of student performance, they also can be a form of evaluation: They can include scores on formal tests on which students reflect, and then set goals for future academic attainment. The key function of portfolios is promoting ongoing assessment: The teacher and student are continually reviewing the contents of the portfolio; there are clear standards and criteria for selection of the most representative artifacts at predetermined times of the year; and student voice, self-reflection, and self-evaluation are always present.

Portfolios promote interaction between students and teachers, students and peers, and students and parents or significant others. The Latin verb *assidere*, from which the word *assess* is derived, is defined as "to sit beside." A well-designed, purposeful, and student-centered portfolio assessment process ensures that teachers and students "sit beside" each other. Teachers find that students who have achieved voice in the portfolio process become active participants in the portfolio assessment process, inviting others to "sit beside them" as they evaluate the outcome and products of their educational experiences.

The notion of a portfolio as a systematic process of students' self-assessment and reflection on what they know, as well as their learning achievement, has gained increasing agreement in recent years. Largely owing to the arrival of the e-portfolio, many educators have developed an interest in student "voice" and self-reflection at the core of the portfolio (Barrett, 2004a). One teacher who has developed expertise in using e-portfolios recognizes that they promote a new, "basic literacy that incorporates technological knowledge, skill and self-reliance and requires that learners are able to demonstrate their knowledge and abilities rather than conform to prescribed evaluation procedures" (Bergmann, 2004, p. 2). Stefanakis (2006) advocates the use of the e-portfolio because students prefer using technology to document what they know. She contends, "[It] enables teachers to work with students at all levels as they place their work into the portfolios throughout the year. In writing, math homework, science lab reports and multimedia work such as music and digital photography [a portfolio] gives a wider range of evidence of their capabilities" (p. 1).

HOW CAN PORTFOLIOS HELP STUDENTS LEARN?

Comparing Work to Past Work Fosters Greater Motivation Than Comparison to the Work of Others

Portfolios as the outcome of a continuous, student-centered process help students learn in a variety of ways. One remarkable by-product of the portfolio process in the classroom is increased student awareness of and responsibility for learning objectives. Since the implementation of the No Child Left Behind (NCLB) federal legislation in the United States, standards for learning and teaching have been raised. The results in terms of classroom life—curricula and instructional practices—have made it mandatory for teachers to address and achieve learning standards for their students. When students are brought into the instructional process through communication of the lesson or unit standards and goals, and when they are given the opportunity to use (or even help create) scoring rubrics that reflect the criteria and levels of achievement required of their performances, they become more motivated to achieve.

Learning Progress Over Time Can Be Clearly Shown

When students know that their portfolio will reflect their growth or skill development over time, they are more focused. They become more rigorous self-evaluators and set goals for their own progress. They value where they have been and how much they have achieved. Because portfolios and e-portfolios include applications of content skills and chronicle students' progress and growth toward meeting curriculum goals and standards, they provide a much richer and more revealing portrait of the student as a learner. Such a picture cannot be captured by a single test score. Within the portfolio process, students become active agents in the acquisition and exposition of their knowledge across the content area of the grade levels.

Portfolios Provide for Clear Communication of Learning Progress to Students, Parents, and Others

If students receive continuous and constructive feedback on the quality of their artifacts, they become more able to self-assess critically. They recognize the power of peer support and become comfortable in inviting peer review. They become able to think flexibly and provide helpful comments to their peers. They grow to appreciate the shared time they spend when their teachers "sit beside" them to share their reflections on the organization and design of their portfolio, as well as the selection of artifacts to be included.

An example of the potential impact and benefits that portfolios and e-portfolios add to student learning is found in the statement of the director of an online portfolio project for high school students in New York state. The project addressed the issue of "student complacency" in a curriculum without authentic assessment and portfolios. "[Students] don't see how their work in school is connected to anything in their lives . . . but collaborating with teachers to build a portfolio gets students involved and leaves them with a product they can be proud of. What's exciting for us is the level of interaction that is happening between teachers and students. Not only are the teachers excited, but also the students are excited about the work. It even helps get parents involved in the process and that's always a good thing" (Teachers College, 2006).

Self-Assessment Skills Are Increased When Students Select the Best Samples of Their Work and Justify Their Choices

Students learn about themselves and the subject they study, "when they are asked to select artifacts for a particular purpose, justify their choices, and make connections across multiple examples, instances, or realms of experience" (Catalyst, 2007). When students actively participate in the portfolio process, it is natural for them to want to know more about how assignments will be structured and graded so they can do their best work. When it comes to problem solving that requires the use of higher-order thinking skills, students who have developed more responsibility in self-assessment are likely to use synthesis and reflection to solve problems, and they are more likely to use their critical and creative thinking skills to select artifacts that best illustrate how a difficult problem was solved.

Focusing on Students' Best Work Provides a Positive Influence on Learning

Portfolios give students the "green light" to do what they seem to do naturally—to save their work. But the process of reflection on goals and standards helps students to become more selective about which pieces of their work will actually become showcased in the portfolio. Sweet (1993) asserts that "portfolios become an effective way to get them to take a second look and think about how they could improve future work. As any teacher or student can confirm, this method is a clear departure from the old write, hand in, and forget mentality, where first drafts were considered final products" (p. 1).

Finally, students' learning is enhanced when they are given opportunities to showcase their portfolios during student-led portfolio conferences for paper portfolios, or to publish their portfolios on school-secured Web sites if they are e-portfolios. When students recognize the audience of "stakeholders" who share their satisfaction and pride in achievement, they become intrinsically motivated to succeed. The advantages of using classroom portfolios are shown in Figure 0.1.

A COMPREHENSIVE ASSESSMENT SYSTEM

Portfolios and e-portfolios can become excellent tools for using the data from both formative (assessment *for*) and summative (assessment *of*) assessment (Catalyst, 2007). A "balanced" or comprehensive assessment system (Figure 0.2) is developed when the portfolio includes three types of assessment in order to arrive at an accurate portrait of a student as a learner: knowledge, processes, and performances. These assessments were asserted by the American Educational Research Association's (AERA's) *Position Statement Concerning High-Stakes Testing,* adopted in July 2000.

The first type of assessment that teachers can include in portfolios and e-portfolios consists of scores from traditional or standardized tests and quizzes.

Advantages of Using Classroom Portfolios

1. Learning progress over time can be clearly shown (e.g., changes in writing skills).

2. Focusing on students' best work provides a positive influence on learning (e.g., best writing samples).

3. Comparing current work to past work fosters greater motivation than comparing one student's work to others' work (e.g., growth in writing skills).

4. Self-assessment skills are increased when students select the best samples of their work and justify their choices (e.g., focus is on criteria of good writing).

5. Portfolios provide for adjustment to individual differences (e.g., students write at their own level but work toward common goals).

6. Portfolios provide for clear communication of learning progress to students, parents, and others (e.g., writing samples obtained at different times can be shown and compared).

Figure 0.1

Balanced Assessment

Type of Assessment	Focus	Features
Traditional	• Knowledge • Curriculum • Skills	Classroom assessments • Tests • Quizzes • Assignments Standardized tests • Norm-referenced • Criterion-referenced
Portfolio	• Process • Product • Growth	• Growth and development • Reflection • Goal setting • Self-evaluation
Performance	• Standards • Application • Transfer	• Collaboration • Tasks • Criteria • Rubrics • Examination of student work

Figure 0.2

Each of these formal, evaluative measures focuses on mastery of students' *knowledge* of the content of curricula. Obviously, this type of assessment is necessary and appropriate, but according to the AERA, the nation's largest professional organization devoted to the scientific study of education, high-stakes testing should not be the sole means of determining a student's success, promotion, or graduation. With respect to the narrow application of test scores in these high-stakes situation, AERA (2007) stresses that

> decisions that affect individual students' life chances or educational opportunities should not be made on the basis of test scores alone. Other relevant information should be taken into account to enhance the overall validity of such decisions. As a minimum assurance of fairness, when tests are used as part of making high-stakes decisions for individual students such as promotion to the next grade or high school graduation, students must be afforded multiple opportunities to pass the test. More importantly, when there is credible evidence that a test score may not adequately reflect a student's true proficiency, alternative acceptable means should be provided by which to demonstrate attainment of the tested standards. (AERA 2007)

The reality for U.S. schools under the federal Elementary and Secondary Education Act–NCLB Title I is that test scores have become the principal criteria by which students, teachers, and school administrators are judged. The use of portfolios and e-portfolios that provide not only qualitative evidence of achievement but also evidence of reflective-statement attachments by students, is important and necessary. Whereas one standardized test score is a single-shot measurement, portfolios and e-portfolios chronicle students' growth and development in a variety of their multiple intelligences, as indicated in the other two types of assessment.

The second type of assessment focuses on the *processes* the student uses to achieve the academic goals. Process assessments tend to provide formative feedback to students and teachers as well as parents while students are learning concepts, knowledge, and skills. Because of this, rough drafts of writing or initial problem-solving strategies should be dated and should include student reflections on how the new piece has improved, and what new ideas, strategies, or concepts have been acquired since the former draft. At the time that the final products are completed, these earlier drafts and reflections are often attached to show growth over time. Portfolios and e-portfolios are highly effective in process assessment because they require students to reflect on their learning, set new goals, and self-evaluate their progress according to known standards.

The third assessment type focuses on student *performances*. Here, students' abilities to apply the knowledge, content, and skills they have learned become evident. Performances allow students to demonstrate that they can transfer the knowledge and skills inherent in the subjects studied into action. These performances often require students to collaborate with peers to create products, projects, or demonstrations according to specific criteria listed in curriculum objectives or learning standards. When students know their performances will be evaluated according to rubrics or scoring guides that provide descriptors for quality work, they become highly engaged in the work. They will take responsibility for the level of achievement in the subject areas, and they and their peers will become interdependent for both feedback and cooperative teamwork to achieve the highest levels of success.

When teachers design portfolio and e-portfolio processes that integrate these three types of assessments, they help meet the individual needs of the students, honor their learning styles, and provide a more accurate evaluation picture of a student's strengths and weaknesses. Portfolios and e-portfolios blend all three types of assessment to attain a developmentally appropriate portrait of a student as a learner. When this is accomplished, teachers attain the goal of implementing the most effective and authentic assessment program for their students.

PORTFOLIOS AND E-PORTFOLIOS CAN BECOME TOOLS FOR CLASSROOM ASSESSMENT OF INDIVIDUAL LEARNERS

One of the most important questions teachers can have regarding portfolios or e-portfolios is how they can authentically assess and reflect on the individual characteristics and achievement of each student. With the growing number of children with special needs who are welcomed into full-inclusion classrooms, there is an increasing need for an assessment system that provides fair, accurate, and helpful information about student progress versus one-dimensional evaluative measures. The Council for Exceptional Children (2007) has recently expressed concerns that we are now "over-emphasizing standardized testing; narrowing curriculum and instruction to focus on test preparation rather than richer academic learning . . . inappropriately excluding low scoring children in order to boost test results; and [providing] inadequate funding. CEC suggest that systems be adopted in order to "make the systemic changes that sustain improved student achievement". Portfolios and e-portfolios have great promise to accomplish this mandate.

Portfolios help diverse students develop deeper insight into and understanding of what they are studying. They also allow teachers to assess the individual students' level of understanding of key concepts because they foster more depth and breadth in the learning process. According to Wiggins and McTighe (1998), going into depth on a topic suggests getting below the surface, and breadth implies the extensions, variety, and connections needed to relate all the separate ideas. Achieving depth and breadth leads students to deeper understanding—and takes more time. This concept will be addressed as we move into Chapters 1 and 2.

PORTFOLIO PROCESSES AND PRODUCTS PROMOTE DIFFERENTIATION

Another important advantage of portfolios and e-portfolios is that they help teachers to differentiate both their teaching process and the products that students create to demonstrate evidence of achievement. If the expression "You get what you assess; and you don't get what you don't assess" is true, then portfolios are imperative in the overall assessment program within the academically diverse classroom. Tomlinson and McTighe (2006) note that

> many educators sense that both teaching and learning have been redirected in ways that are potentially impoverishing for those who teach and those who learn. . . . Educators need a model that acknowledges the centrality of standards but that also demonstrates how meaning and understanding can both emanate from and frame content standards so that young people develop powers of mind. (p. 1)

Portfolios and e-portfolios can assist teachers in creating these models while also engaging students in both critical and creative thinking. Portfolios provide students with multiple strategies for constructing meaning from information and experiences, and for demonstrating their mastery of standards. Teachers acquire a viable method for differentiating learning and assessment to meet the diverse needs of their students when portfolios and e-portfolios are used.

AUTHENTIC LEARNING AND ASSESSMENT

One of the keys to a successful portfolio system includes using a variety of authentic assessments. The portfolio would be no different from a working folder if it included only tests, quizzes, work sheets, and homework assignments. Authentic assessment focuses on each student's ability to produce quality products and performances. It also places the student at the heart of assessment as a critic and evaluator of the work completed.

As previously shown, portfolios and e-portfolios become effective tools for classroom assessment of individual learners, including those with learning needs or challenges. They also can be used by groups or teams of learners who seek to compare their performance or academic tasks to the standards or benchmarks placed before them. Authentic assessments provide the context for portfolio process development when they highlight the criteria for what should be included.

REPERTOIRE OF ASSESSMENTS

The portfolio provides a fully realized portrait of the student as a learner because it utilizes a rich palette of assessment tools. A standardized test or teacher-made test, by contrast, will likely emphasize only verbal/linguistic and logical/mathematical skills. A portfolio and e-portfolio can showcase students' multiple intelligences by including artifacts that also reflect their visual/spatial, musical/rhythmic, interpersonal, intrapersonal, bodily/kinesthetic, and naturalist intelligences (Gardner 1983, 1993). The well-designed academic portfolio will contain assessment tools that have engaged students in multiple media and multiple opportunities to showcase their academic learning (Figure 0.3).

Assessment Tools

Assessment	Evaluation
• Ongoing • Collection of data • Formative	• Final judgment • End result • Summative
Authentic Assessment	**Portfolio**
• Meaningful tasks • Self-assessment • Application	• Collection of evidence • Growth and development • Framework for learning

Figure 0.3

Self-Assessment—The Power of Reflection

The genuine power of the portfolio emerges when students analyze and describe the work they include, discuss the key concepts they have learned, and, most important, reflect on how this learning has affected them. A portfolio is really a multisensory and multidimensional personification of a student's entire learning process and learning dispositions. Without the engagement of students in self-reflection, self-assessment, and evaluation of their work against known standards, the emergence of student voice is limited. If students merely collect and store work in a paper or electronic folder, the effectiveness of using the work as evidence of achievement is minimized. It is the critical element of reflection that fosters the higher-order critical thinking and decision-making skills necessary for continuous learning and improvement. *Self-assessment* describes the entire process by which students develop judgments and perception of *what* has been learned. While self-assessing, students analyze products and the outcomes of performances and compare them to the known standards or criteria, or both. The student, like the artist, will use a palette of media and processes that showcase his or her individuality, achievement, and uniqueness (Figure 0.4).

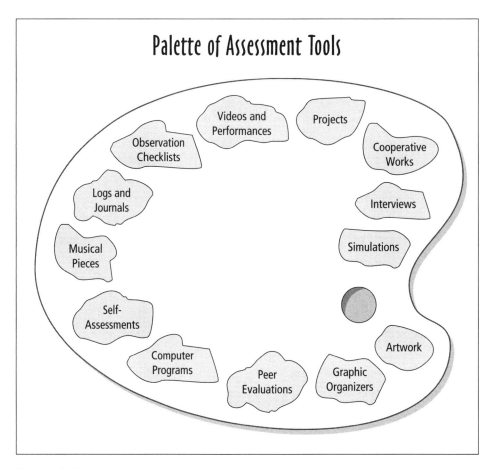

Figure 0.4

Figure 0.5 illustrates the variety of performance and product assessments that a student would likely include in the portfolio or e-portfolio. The *self-evaluation* promoted by the portfolio process engages students in acquiring an understanding of

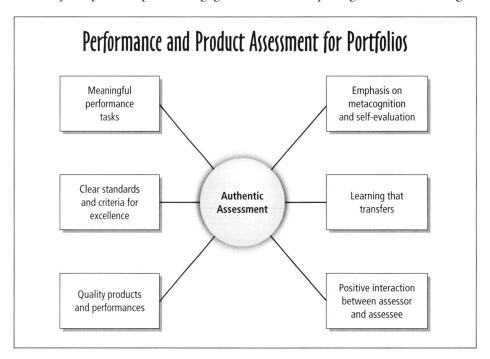

Figure 0.5

how they are learning, as opposed to *what* they are learning. It is the means for the students to make significant strides in understanding themselves as learners.

Regular opportunity to engage in self-reflection becomes the heart and soul of the portfolio process because it enhances learners' ability to assess their work and analyze strengths and weaknesses. From this process, they are able to set new goals for growth. It has been noted that strength in self-reflection leads to "voice," and that this is a prerequisite to the development of human agency. Schools striving to meet the challenge of preparing students to become active participants in democracy must develop *human agency*—the capacity for human beings to make choices and apply them in the world for the good of all. In his book *Motivation and Agency,* Mele (2005) draws a correlation between human agency and motivation. Portfolio and e-portfolio reflective processes that promote student voice also address this important development of agency.

The process known as metacognition, or "thinking about one's thinking," is the mental skill required of students for a successful portfolio or e-portfolio. Through this process, the students take control of their learning by becoming informed critics of their own work. Teachers and parents often serve as "guides on the side," but the students themselves are supported in the portfolio process. While assisting students in refining their work. the process of metacognition also builds within them the capacity to self-assess and redirect their efforts. Costa and Kallick (1992) suggest that "we must constantly remind ourselves that the ultimate purpose of evaluation is to have students become self-evaluating. If students graduate from our schools still dependent upon others to tell them when they are adequate, good, or excellent, then we have missed the whole point of what education is about" (p. 280).

THE PORTFOLIO PROCESS

The richness of the portfolio and e-portfolio as a container of valuable assessment tools is often evident to educators, but the reality is that implementing an effective portfolio system is very time consuming. The collection of student work, the selection of key items, and periodic reviews that engage students in evaluation of their progress all require considerable time and effort by students and teachers. It is no wonder that there are several questions raised by educators before considering the use of portfolio and e-portfolio processes. The following are questions that will be addressed in *The Portfolio Connection:*

1. What is a portfolio? What is an e-portfolio? What is a portfolio for?

2. How does it a portfolio or e-portfolio work? How do you "do" it?

3. Where do you start?

4. How do you adapt the portfolio to different ages and stages of learners?

5. What do you need to know before, during, and at the conclusion of the portfolio process?

6. How do you tie a portfolio to standards or local and state curricula?

7. How do you make sure that students are connected to the purpose of the portfolio? How do you make sure portfolios showcase their achievements?

8. What are the teaching and assessment tools you need to know about before beginning the portfolio process?

9. What are the procedures you need to follow in order to have successful student-led conferences and showcases?

These are just some of the organizational questions that must be answered before and during the process of the portfolio journey. But as wtih any journey, it is important to understand that it is the *process* and the *viewpoint* along the way—and not simply the end product—that provide the wonderment, learning, and recall that are intrinsic to life. This book will serve as a guide to the teachers, students, school administrators, and parents embarking on portfolio and e-portfolio assessment. It will become clear as the chapters progress that there are no right answers to these questions, since each teaching and learning situation is different. This book will help each reader explore the ideas and activities to be considered in order to create a workable portfolio or e-portfolio system that is intrinsically satisfying and motivating to all students. Each chapter will provide helpful tips and ideas for developing portfolios as accurate accountability processes for teachers and school administrators, while also enhancing diverse students' motivation, performance, and voice. An outline of the chapters in *The Portfolio Connection* appears below followed by a brief summary of each section.

Chapter 1: Connect Portfolio Purpose to Audience	1. What is a portfolio? What is an e-portfolio? What is it used for? Who is it for? Does it promote differentiation in the curriculum and classroom instruction?
Chapter 2: Connect Portfolio Design to Developmental Stages	2. How does it work? How do you do it? Where do you start? How do you adapt the portfolio to different ages and stages of learners? How do you adapt the e-portfolio to students' emergent through proficient technology levels?
Chapter 3: Connect Portfolio Content to Local and State Standards and Curricula	3. What do you need to know in order to tie student portfolios to local and state standards or curricula? What is the difference between assessment *of* and assessment *for* learning? What are the assessment tools that motivate students and promote accountability for learners and evidence of achievement for teachers?
Chapter 4: Connect to Portfolio Purpose Through Students' Collections, Reflections, and Selections	4. How do you ensure that students become "connected" to the purpose of the portfolio and can self-assess the work to be selected and included? How are portfolios and e-portfolios organized?
Chapter 5: Connect Students' Reflection and Self-Assessment to Criteria, Rubrics, and Standards	5. What are the tools needed to prepare students to effectively self-assess and use benchmarks of achievements? How have different states and countries succeeded in using portfolios to promote student success?
Chapter 6: Connect Students' Voices Through Web Conferences and Showcases	6. What are the procedures needed to prepare students for final portfolio events—peer portfolio conferences, academic conferences, and showcases? What are the procedures needed to prepare students for online e-portfolio events—peer portfolio conferences or Web showcases?

CHAPTER 1: CONNECT PORTFOLIO PURPOSE TO AUDIENCE

Before embarking on the design of a portfolio or e-portfolio process, it is critical to know what the portfolio can do, and for whom. Understanding what portfolios are and how they work as either print collections or electronic compendia of student work is necessary in order to plan for a process that truly connects students to their work, their learning standards, and the audience(s) who are invested in the students' success. As we have said earlier, portfolios and e-portfolios exist at the intersection of student evaluation and self-assessment. This means that the student becomes the principal voice of the portfolio process while teachers, parents, and local school administrators contribute to its construction. State—and now federal (under NCLB)—policymakers are also included as important audiences or stakeholders in the evidence and outcomes of student achievement that can be found in academic portfolios. This chapter will focus on establishing a basic knowledge of portfolios and e-portfolios, defining their purposes, and discussing how they can be used. It will also discuss why they need to be designed and implemented in ways that meet the diverse needs and abilities of students, while also serving to inform the various audiences concerned with the education of children.

CHAPTER 2: CONNECT PORTFOLIO DESIGN TO DEVELOPMENTAL STAGES

Before designing an effective portfolio or e-portfolio process that will be comprehensible as well as satisfying to students, teachers need to consider the developmental stages of the students they teach. For e-portfolios, it is additionally important for teachers to consider the technological ability of their students and determine what skills they may need to develop before proceeding. Understanding that an effective portfolio process is one in which students (and their parents or guardians) are highly involved from the outset will also enable the teacher to determine what knowledge, skills, and dispositions students will need to possess or develop along the way.

After the portfolio or e-portfolio purposes are developed, the next step is to clearly communicate them to students and parents. Although working with teams of teachers by grade level or with schoolwide staff and administrators is more efficacious, teachers themselves can establish a developmentally appropriate portfolio process (and the authentic assessment procedures that support it) on their own. As with teaching, considering the learning needs of the students and the best ways in which they acquire knowledge is vital to the successful design and implementation of portfolios and e-portfolios. This chapter will provide guidelines on how to get started and what decisions to make in order to communicate effectively what will need to be accomplished to students and parents. It will also provide suggestions and tools for adapting the portfolio to different ages and stages of learners.

CHAPTER 3: CONNECT PORTFOLIO CONTENT TO LOCAL AND STATE STANDARDS AND CURRICULA

Standards-based portfolios provide evidence of teacher and student accountability. When portfolio artifacts are correlated to district or state curricular content and performance standards, teachers assist students in submitting documentation that the standards have been addressed, met, or exceeded, and that provide evidence of students' progress toward meeting or exceeding the standards.

When considering the use of portfolios and e-portfolios that align with standards, teachers often need to consult their school's or district's policies regarding assessment. Since portfolios can play an effective part in a comprehensive assessment system for districts or for individual public or private schools, the processes found in this book regarding design, student voice, self-assessment, and evaluation are critically important considerations to be made.

This chapter will address issues of how schools can begin to develop portfolio or e-portfolio systems that show evidence of student learning over time. Ideas from different states in the United States that have linked portfolios to standards and curricular goals will be provided. In addition, this chapter will discuss what needs to be done by principals, teachers, and students if portfolios are to support student achievement and promote parent involvement. Discussion of the portfolio's shift toward the student in "assessment for" learning will be provided. Finally, this chapter will include some insights from the international community's development of model portfolio systems.

CHAPTER 4: CONNECT PORTFOLIO PURPOSE THROUGH STUDENTS' COLLECTIONS, REFLECTIONS, AND SELECTIONS

Teachers are responsible for covering the content and processes in their curriculum. Sometimes the curriculum uses a scope and sequence organization, and other times it lists the content pieces to be addressed in each grade level or course. Knowledge of content can become a principal purpose of the portfolio. Using content to demonstrate processes such as writing, speaking, and problem solving could be another purpose. In most cases, teachers integrate content and process to provide evidence of knowledge and application of knowledge.

This chapter will address the important question of making sure that students and their parents feel connected to the purpose of the portfolio and have regular opportunities to self-assess and evaluate the work that is selected and included. It will provide insight on how portfolios and e-portfolios can be organized to achieve their purposes.

CHAPTER 5: CONNECT STUDENTS' REFLECTION AND SELF-ASSESSMENT TO CRITERIA, RUBRICS, AND STANDARDS

Pieces or artifacts in the portfolio or e-portfolio will show how students meet the pre-determined goals and purposes. Because students need to know these purposes before engaging in the portfolio process, criteria and procedures must be developed to help them determine what should be selected from what is often referred to as the working folder. The portfolio and e-portfolio will include only the items that provide evidence of meeting the goals and addressing the purpose of the portfolio. Here, the "less is more" philosophy guides the portfolio development. This chapter will present the tools needed to engage students in both learning and assessment, and will discuss how to continually develop and clarify the portfolio or e-portfolio purpose. Experience has told us that when purpose is clearly and coherently known by the students (and their parents), students are empowered to "selectively abandon" any work that does not measure up or adequately address the goals and purposes.

Many of the portfolio or e-portfolio entries will include products from projects and performances. Therefore, teachers will need to become skillful in creating criteria checklists and scoring rubrics that provide the specific indicators that students need to master in order to perform successfully on each assignment. With criteria checklists and rubrics, students can assess their own work as well as assist peers in determining if they meet the benchmarks and criteria. Parents, too, can review work their students have completed while using the authentic assessments that accompany them. Teachers can also use checklists to monitor student work and provide assistance throughout the process. This ongoing, formative feedback during the inspection stage can lead to marked improvement in the quality of student work.

Since students' reflection is the heart and soul of portfolios, they need to be encouraged to write reflections about what they have learned, how they have learned it, and what insight they have gained about their learning and themselves. These self-authored descriptions of their work help teachers and parents get a better understanding of whether or not they have grasped the important concepts of the learning. More important, the reflections reveal how students have internalized the learning and connected it with their lives. In addition to providing ideas about introducing and norming various tools for authentic assessment, this chapter presents the procedures needed to prepare students for culminating portfolio events—online Web showcase, peer portfolio conferences, and academic showcases.

CHAPTER 6: CONNECT STUDENTS' VOICES THROUGH WEB CONFERENCES AND SHOWCASES

Through regular and ongoing reflection and self-evaluation, students come to value their work as representing who they are and what they can do. Even though the students may have done their very best work, they still need to prepare for the essence of portfolios—the communication and acknowledgment of who they are as learners. At the last stage of the portfolio development process, students are given the opportunity to showcase or give voice to who they have become as learners. They are given the opportunity to show how they have met or exceeded standards and how they have achieved the purposes of the portfolio. Artifacts showing "clear and compelling " evidence of achieving standards in the subject areas are enhanced when students take another reflective stance and reveal their perceptions and attitudes about the effort expended and the outcomes derived from learning. Parents and others are invited to view evidence in the portfolio or e-portfolio that tells the story of how and why students have met curriculum goals and standards.

This chapter describes how the portfolio conference or online showcase helps teachers, parents, and students talk about the learning context and content. The conversations related to student work provide valuable insights into the students' understanding. They also invite discussions about alternative strategies for meeting academic goals. Portfolio exhibitions and showcases celebrate learning by allowing people other than the teacher and parent to view and respond to the story of each student's learning. The procedures, tools, and reflections that comprise this important part of portfolios will be provided throughout the chapter.

1

Connect Portfolio Purpose to Audience

What would motivate teachers to undertake a portfolio assessment system when they are already overwhelmed by mandates to raise test scores, cover all the objectives provided in four-inch-thick curriculum guides, and manage the behavior of culturally, academically, physically, and socially diverse students? The thrill of victory? The desire for greatness? The love of a challenge? The search for something to fill class time? The answer is that most teachers instinctively believe they are worth the effort, even though portfolios present many organizational and time-management challenges. Teachers recognize that academic portfolios promote assessment for and provide evidence of learning. When teachers engage their students in the processes that are inherent in the portfolio process, students develop a better awareness and knowledge of curricular goals and standards. Teachers, like many parents and students, recognize that standardized tests used as a single measure of student achievement are not accurate representations of many students' true capabilities. They are searching for ways to meet the needs of students from diverse cultures, with diverse values, individual learning abilities, and multidimensional learning styles. Glazer (1998) says that many assessment procedures have been insensitive to the diversity found in classrooms as a result of people's misunderstanding of assessment and evaluation. She warns that "for most, tests, testing, and the resulting test scores prevail as indicators of achievement" (p. 20). Glazer also believes that, by selecting appropriate assessment tools and instructional strategies, teachers can respect the originality each student brings to a classroom. The academic portfolio brings together these tools and strategies as it provides a framework that encourages students to showcase their individuality and originality within the context of the classroom.

Instruction is assessment, and assessment is instruction. As Paulson, Paulson, and Meyer (1991) put it, "[Portfolios] can be powerful educational tools for encouraging students to take charge of their learning. . . . If carefully assembled, portfolios become an intersection of instruction and assessment; they are not *just* instruction or *just* assessment, but, rather, both. Together, instruction and assessment give more than either give separately" (p. 61; emphasis in original).

WHY USE PORTFOLIOS?

Portfolios provide information about a student that traditional paper-and-pencil tests cannot. They present a demonstration of the student's academic skills and learning dispositions that helps teachers, students, and parents make informal decisions about instruction. Portfolios and e-portfolios have been especially helpful in representing the achievement and progress of students with special needs. Several states, including Kentucky, Tennessee, and Vermont, have incorporated portfolio processes as alternatives to formal assessment for many of their students receiving special school services. Under the federal No Child Left Behind legislation, more states and school districts mandate testing programs to gather data about student achievement. These data are used to hold schools, teachers, and students accountable. (See Figure 1.1 for reasons that support use of portfolios.) Yet dependence on testing alone can lead to curriculum and instruction bereft of meaningfulness or dimension. Educators who strive to learn about all their students and who promote success for each of them have turned to portfolios and e-portfolios as tools that bring the disparate elements of curriculum together in a satisfying manner for all concerned.

WHAT IS A PORTFOLIO?

Carr and Harris (2001) describe an academic portfolio as a "purposeful, integrated collection of student work showing effort, progress, or achievement in one or more areas. . . . Assessment is enhanced when students select the items for their portfolios, [their] self-reflection is encouraged, and criteria for success are clear" (p. 181). For this reason, portfolios are among the most frequently mentioned tools for promoting student voice. When committed to using portfolio systems, the use of authentic assessment in the classroom becomes as important as testing. In her book *Power of Portfolios*, Hebert (2001) refers to portfolios as "modern memory boxes" (p. x). While portfolios can and do become important collections of key "artifacts" that remind students of their growth over time and of their accomplishment of learning standards, they also provide a deep, rich anthology of learning evidence.

WHAT IS AN E-PORTFOLIO?

As technology and telecommunication tools have been acquired in elementary and secondary schools, the e-portfolio has proven to be a powerful vehicle for

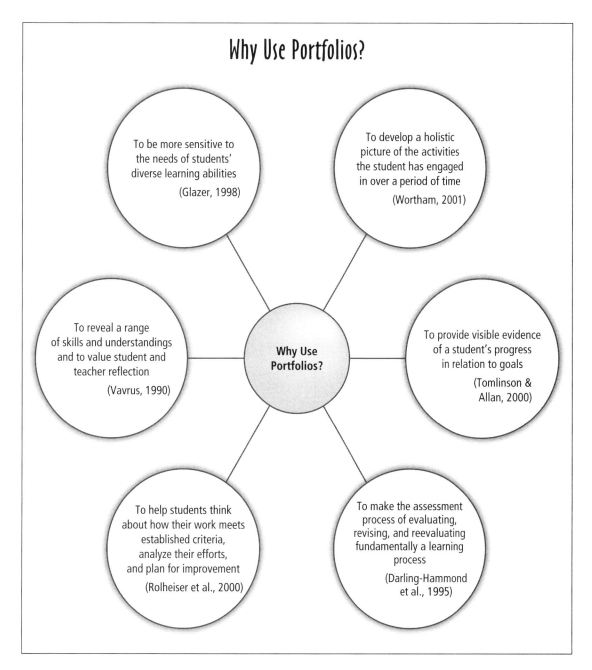

Figure 1.1

promoting both student engagement and voice in the learning process. Batson (2002) describes the e-portfolio as a collection of student work that brings together three trends: the electronic form of much student work, especially at the upper-grade or secondary levels; the availability of the Internet, where students can both access and produce information; and accessibility of databases that allow students to manage large volumes of their work. The e-portfolio offers a multimedia dimension to the portfolio that "allows the creator to present learning and reflective artifacts in a variety of media formats (audio, graphics, video, and text)" (Montgomery & Wiley, 2004, p. 5). In a recent call for papers, the Technology, Communication, and Literacy Committee of the International Reading Association declared

> the electronic portfolio has emerged as a logical next step in the evolution of portfolio assessment. Regardless of the technology employed or the institutional context, the electronic portfolio offers several pragmatic features not available with traditional paper-based portfolio assessments:
>> —*Ease of storing and archiving artifacts.* The electronic portfolio makes it feasible to archive massive amounts of data. For the first time in the history of educational assessment, it is practical to review a comprehensive set of student work samples collected over years. From audio passages of students reading aloud to writing samples and projects, electronic portfolios offer educators access to documentation of student learning that goes well beyond anything that could be captured in the manila cumulative folder.
>> —*The inclusion of multimedia artifacts.* The electronic portfolio allows for powerful additions to the historical record of student learning and teacher professional development through the integration of audio and video texts.
>> —The possibility that the nonlinear nature of electronic documents will encourage reflection that connects disparate artifacts and learning experiences in unique ways. (International Reading Association, 2004)

HOW IS A PORTFOLIO USED?

Portfolios and e-portfolios can be used in many different ways according to the purposes that are determined by teachers and administrators. A primary purpose for the use of portfolios in schools is to "assess student performance through authentic work in the same way professionals demonstrate their abilities by compiling samples of work in a portfolio" (Ash, 2000, p. 11). As for digital or e-portfolios, most simply put, the e-portfolio is "a 'hypermedia' document [composed of] a set of screens or pages, in the terminology of the software, that are linked by buttons on the screen. When the user clicks the mouse to select a button, the program reacts, typically by navigating to another screen or by showing some additional information" (Niquida, 1993, p. 3).

Who Is It For?

The establishment of *purpose* is the foundation of portfolios and e-portfolios. It involves decisions not only about how the portfolio will be used but also for whom the portfolio will be developed. In most instances, portfolios will simply be developed for students, parents, and teachers. Increasingly, however, the audience for portfolios has grown to include school administrators, district leaders, state officials, and the larger public.

When portfolios or e-portfolios are under consideration by teachers and school leaders, it is important to place students at the center of the process. As the use of test scores and the testing industry itself have dramatically increased, it has become clear that students (and their work and achievements) are too often reduced to a set of test scores. Portfolios and e-portfolios have the power to offset the detrimental effects on students in working only for a grade and on teachers in teaching only to the test. Smith (1999) comments on the statewide portfolio system that was earlier employed in Vermont:

> Students hold the key to much of what they know and are able to do. They understand their strengths, and they can identify the things that challenge them. Too often, however, they are the last people consulted in developing procedures or practices for the assessment of their own learning. Too often the procedures and practices we do employ to measure student learning focus on instant recall of prescribed information. Rarely do they measure what students truly understand about themselves and their learning. Rarely do students have the opportunity to reflect on their own learning and growth, and rarely are they asked to use what they know and are able to do to demonstrate that growth and understanding. (p. 1)

Designing portfolios as ways to promote student achievement and assessment *for* learning is central to this book. In Figure 1.2, Barrett (2002) delineates the characteristic differences between assessment of and assessment for learning.

ASSESSMENT *FOR* LEARNING VERSUS ASSESSMENT *OF* LEARNING

Portfolios promote formative assessment for improving student learning	Portfolios show summative evidence of student learning
Students (and parents) are invited by teachers to participate in determining purposes of portfolios.	Portfolio purposes are aligned with local, state or national mandates.
Students know the portfolio tells the story of how, when and why they are learning,	Formal tests, unit examinations, standardized assessments as determined by the school, district, state, etc.
Students understand that their portfolio changes and they grow, learn and achieve,	Portfolios usually tied to "high-stakes" examinations or performances,
Students and parents have opportunities to select, inspect and reflect on entries included in portfolios.	Standard scoring rubrics are normed for portfolio readers and each portfolio is rated accordingly.
Students have voice in the collection and selection of portfolio artifacts throughout the year.	Portfolio content, organization and selection criteria are determined at the school, district, state or national level.
Portfolios assist students, their teachers and parents in making developmental decisions about future learning goals.	Portfolios only provide artifacts of evidence that shows what has been learned.
Portfolios promote student motivation because they include student voice, decision making and self-assessment.	Portfolios provide extrinsic motivation to either achieve learning standards.
Portfolios provide an opportunity for students to celebrate learning by inviting a variety of audiences to view their content.	Portfolios become anonymous and are often read by external audiences who are unfamiliar with students.

Figure 1.2

Throughout this and subsequent chapters, we will assist teachers and other portfolio designers in establishing the principal purposes for portfolios and e-portfolios that will effectively promote formative *assessment of* the student, and summative *assessment for* learning while promoting student voice.

Defining Portfolio Purpose

Before introducing students to portfolios as meaningful containers or compendia of assessment products, it is critical that teachers study the "big picture" and determine the primary and secondary functions of the portfolio or e-portfolio. Teachers need answers to the following frequently asked questions:

- How can academic portfolios be used?
- How will they support teaching goals and learning objectives?
- Who, other than the students and teachers, will be the audiences?
- How will students become aware of the purposes of the portfolios?
- What available technologies should support selection of e-portfolios?
- How will students become involved in the ongoing portfolio assessment processes?
- How will portfolios or e-portfolios be organized?
- How will portfolios or e-portfolios be shared with the identified audience, and how will these audiences be effectively involved?
- How will portfolios ensure differentiation in the curriculum and classroom instruction for diverse learners' needs and learning challenges?

INTRODUCTION

"Portfolios have the potential to reveal a good deal about their creators. They can become a window into students' minds, a means for both staff and students to understand the educational process at the level of the individual learner. They can be powerful educational tools for encouraging students to take charge of their own learning" (Paulson et al., 1991, p. 61; see also Figure 1.3, this volume). E-portfolios can integrate student learning achievement of standards with the use of the multimedia tools that today's technology offers. These forms of portfolios are capable of providing an even more complete portrait of students as learners. Stefanakis (2002) makes a strong case for the use of districtwide portfolios and e-portfolios as the basis of comprehensive assessment systems: "The goal for each district is to carefully construct a comprehensive assessment system, with a collection of assessments that allow many stakeholders to use these data to improve both student learning and teachers' teaching. Without portfolios to make visible what students do and what teachers teach, I am not sure this can be done" (p. 137).

An increasing number of teachers who have successfully used portfolios have discovered the power of telecommunication tools to develop, review, and showcase students' achievements. The joining of computer-technology applications and the Internet, along with the communication power of the academic or developmental portfolio, has allowed today's educators to achieve both learning goals and assessment goals.

Figure 1.3

PORTFOLIO PURPOSES

Determining the purpose of the portfolio or e-portfolio and its function in promoting and showcasing student performance is perhaps the most important part of the process. It essentially creates the "big picture," or canvas, on which students will project their voice, goals, achievements, and skills.

The purposes for the portfolio and e-portfolio must be carefully determined by the teacher or instructional team before the portfolio process begins. Following are a number of purposes that teachers and portfolio designers might select as primary or secondary uses for portfolios and e-portfolios. (See Blacklines 1.1, 1.2, and 1.3 at the end of this chapter.)

- *Learning portfolios:* to capture evidence of students' acquisition of knowledge and skill over time—evidence that demonstrates both content and process knowledge.
- *Developmental portfolios:* to demonstrate the continuing growth and development of students as readers, writers, mathematical problem solvers, and so on, over time. These portfolios are often used for special-needs students because they are effective in "telling the story" of the student as a unique person and learner.

- *Assessment/standards portfolios:* to demonstrate clear and compelling evidence of student achievement and proficiency, as compared to single or multiple subject standards.
- *Showcase portfolios* (*best work*): to provide exemplars of distinguished or best student work or performances.

Regardless of the purpose, it is important to remember that portfolios are *more* than products that students submit in order to fulfill academic requirements or to meet learning benchmarks. They contain much less than a *working folder* in which students place all their work. A portfolio or e-portfolio is part of an ongoing reflective process that enables students to analyze and self-assess their performances and learning dispositions. If teachers keep that in mind, the establishment of the portfolio purpose can ensure that students are able to acquire subject area knowledge while becoming active and thoughtful learners.

The Learning Portfolio

The purpose of the learning portfolio is to capture the processes of student learning. It engages the student in selecting pieces or "artifacts" that demonstrate content and process knowledge over time. Since most classes today are heterogeneously grouped, the work selected for a learning portfolio will document the entry point of each student. This documentation supplies the baseline data that are necessary to measure growth over time. When this is the purpose, students select artifacts at the beginning of the year, or at the point the student enters the class. The subsequent selection of items throughout the year for the portfolio or e-portfolio essentially "tracks" the student's progress in a subject area and the learning processes that support it. These portfolios become running records of students' progress over time, which helps students to recognize their own strengths and weaknesses. They motivate students to set goals for improvement and attainment of benchmarks. (See Blackline 1.9 at the end of this chapter.)

Important benefits of learning portfolios are that they can be designed to accommodate all students' diversity and that they allow students to demonstrate their individual learning and achievement through a wide variety of authentic learning situations.

The Developmental Portfolio

In order to ensure optimal learning experiences for all students, including those with special needs, the developmental portfolio can be used to demonstrate the continuing growth and development of students as readers, writers, mathematical problem solvers, and so on, over time. The purpose of this portfolio or e-portfolio is to provide fair, accurate, and helpful information about student progress in a multidimensional way. It promotes student engagement in selection and reflection on work over time, and includes dated entries that provide a portrait of a "learner in motion." Students, parents, and teachers are able to "monitor" academic and social growth throughout the year with this type of portfolio. This portfolio might take the form of an autobiography or a best work portfolio where the students' goals are to tell the story of themselves as unique individuals and learners. (See Blackline 1.8 at the end of this chapter.)

Teachers of prekindergarten and early primary children often use "learning lists" to assist children in looking at early and current work and in establishing goals. They might interview the young child while the child looks at portfolio pieces. Preliterate children can dictate their responses as they view items in this portfolio: "One thing I am good at . . ." "One thing I am having trouble with . . ." "One thing I know . . ." Elementary children use learning lists, learning logs, and journals to supplement the reflection and self-assessment that the developmental portfolio promotes. Secondary level students show how they have progressed in acquiring new abilities in foreign languages, the arts, or technology through a developmental portfolio. These types of portfolios or e-portfolios become running records of students' progress over time while helping them and their audience recognize their strengths and set goals to strengthen weaknesses.

Assessment/Evaluative Portfolio

Also known at the *standards-based portfolio,* the purpose of the assessment/ evaluative portfolio is to demonstrate single or multiple subject-area knowledge and skills at key predetermined points in the academic year. Artifacts selected for this portfolio provide evidence of levels of knowledge in mathematics, language arts, science, art, music, or vocational education. The items contained in this portfolio indicate evidence of not only passive student knowledge but also the *application* of that knowledge through action and performances—written work, group presentations, lesson products, multimedia presentations, and other projects. Students select, reflect on, and self-assess these artifacts to provide evidence that they have demonstrated and applied content knowledge and skill that meets (or exceeds) known standards or benchmarks. (See Blackline 1.6 at the end of this chapter.)

An important aspect of student engagement in this evaluative portfolio is the ability to develop perspective about the importance of ongoing assessment. Students recognize the relevance of each artifact and set goals for how the knowledge it portrays will be used in lifelong learning skills such as writing, reading, problem solving, and decision making. The standards-based portfolio is an important tool for promoting student voice in curriculum as well as assessment. Typical tools that teachers develop and utilize with this portfolio are checklists, performance rubrics, learning logs, and, of course, tests and quizzes.

When teachers promote the reflective stance for students who are maintaining their standards portfolio or e-portfolio, students begin to take more responsibility for and engagement in the direction of their own learning. They are able to set and reach goals for achievement and skill building as they recognize how their performance and knowledge compare to the learning outcomes and standards that are regularly provided to them. (See Example 1.5 at the end of this chapter.) Once key purposes are in place, the process of implementing an effective portfolio system begins.

TYPES OF PORTFOLIOS

Once purpose is established, teachers, parents, administrators, and district decision makers can jointly study the portfolio's or e-portfolio's anticipated impact and develop policies that promote student learning while protecting student confidentiality and individuality. (This protection is especially necessary when technology is available and the decision is made to promote e-portfolios.) Teachers and other portfolio designers then consider the type of portfolio that can best achieve these purposes. The following portfolio types used by themselves or in combination with other ideas can fulfill the purposes of most academic portfolios. These types can be classified into two categories: personal and academic. A subcategory of each of these categories is group portfolios, which many educators find to be worthwhile for promoting interdependence and a strong sense of community in the classroom.

PERSONAL PORTFOLIOS

Showcase Portfolios (Electronic Scrapbooks)

Items from outside school are included in this portfolio or e-portfolio to form a holistic picture of the students. This portfolio focuses on students' hobbies, community activities, musical or artistic talents, sports, families, pets, or travels. Artifacts include pictures, awards, videos, and memorabilia.

Multiple Intelligences Portfolios

Schools seeking to ensure the success of students with diverse needs and learning styles implement the multiple intelligences portfolios to showcase all aspects of the students' gifts and talents. The portfolios might include activities and assessments based on Gardner's (1983, 1993) multiple intelligences: visual/spatial, logical/mathematical, verbal/linguistic, musical/rhythmic, interpersonal, intrapersonal, bodily/kinesthetic, and naturalist. Students who are empowered to make their own choices will include paper-based entries, as well as a variety of entries such as visuals, digital recordings, videotapes, and pictures to showcase their abilities and personalities (Figure 1.4). This portfolio helps classmates, teachers, and others get to know students and join them in a celebration of their interests and successes outside the traditional confines of school. (See Example 1.4 at the end of this chapter.)

Autobiographical Portfolios

Students can also develop a written or multimedia portfolio that becomes an autobiographical portfolio. Preprimary and primary children might construct a portfolio of family members and important family events. Intermediate and middle school children enjoy putting together portfolios of family, friends, pets, favorite activities, and awards. High school students might include all of the above, as well as college or career goals, future travel or family plans, and reflections on what they need to accomplish to make their dreams a reality. (See Example 1.2 and Blackline 1.10 at the end of this chapter.)

Intelligent Behaviors Portfolios

Teachers promoting intelligent and socially responsible behaviors for students within their classrooms can develop portfolios that help students focus

Multiple Intelligence Portfolio

Visual/Spatial
Images, graphics, drawings, sketches, maps, charts, doodles, pictures, spatial orientation, puzzles, designs, looks, appeal, mind's eye, imagination, visualization, dreams, nightmares, films, and videos

Logical/Mathematical
Reasoning, deductive and inductive logic, facts, data, information, spreadsheets, databases, sequencing, ranking, organizing, analyzing, proofs, conclusions, judging, evaluations, and assessments

Verbal/Linguistic
Words, wordsmiths, speaking, writing, listening, reading, papers, essays, poems, plays, narratives, lyrics, spelling, grammar, foreign languages, memos, bulletins, newsletters, newspapers, e-mail, faxes, speeches, talks, dialogues, and debates

Musical/Rhythmic
Music, rhythm, beat, melody, tunes, allegro, pacing, timbre, tenor, soprano, opera, baritone, symphony, choir, chorus, madrigals, rap, rock, rhythm and blues, jazz, classical, folk, ads and jingles

Bodily/Kinesthetic
Activity, action, experiental, hands-on, experiments, try, do, perform, play, drama, sports, throw, toss, catch, jump, twist, twirl, assemble, disassemble, form, re-form, manipulate, touch, feel, immerse, and participate

Interpersonal
Interact, communicate, converse, share understand, empathize, sympathize, reach out, care, talk, whisper, laugh, cry, shudder, socialize, meet, greet, lead, follow, gangs, clubs, charisma, crowds, gatherings, and twosomes

Interpersonal
Self, solitude, meditate, think, create, brood, reflect, envision, journal, self-assess, set goals, plot, plan, dream, write, fiction, nonfiction, poetry, affirmations, lyrics, songs, screenplays, commentaries, introspection, and inspection

Naturalist
Nature, natural, environment, listen, watch, observe, classify, categorize, discern patterns, appreciate, hike, climb, fish, hunt, dive, photograph, trees, leaves, animals, living things, flora, fauna, ecosystem, sky, grass, mountains, lakes, and rivers

Figure 1.4

SOURCE: Adapted from Fogarty and Stoehr, 1995, p. 8.

on these behaviors throughout an academic year. Intelligent behaviors include evidence of persistence; empathic listening; and flexibility in thinking, metacognitive awareness, problem posing, and problem solving (Costa, 1991). These behaviors transcend content areas and highlight dispositions that transfer to the students' lives away from school. When teachers know that "you get what you assess and you don't get what you don't assess" (Bass, 1993, p. 32), they recognize the use of intelligent behavior portfolios as an effective learning and assessment process in promoting students' development into successful and thoughtful young adults.

Portphotos

Adelman (2007) describes how the use of portfolios of photographs (portphotos) enhances students' learning while promoting an authentic review of their work. By using photographs of completed projects or videos of student performances, individual students are able to create a progress portfolio that resembles an "autobiography of a work." Adelman has successfully used this media to promote student motivation and reflection in sustained learning within subjects such as social studies, science, and mathematics. (See Example 1.6 at the end of this chapter.)

ACADEMIC PORTFOLIOS

Standards Portfolio

The standards portfolio is becoming more necessary as a means of documenting students' academic achievement and ensuring teacher participation in the student assessment process. Academic portfolios and e-portfolios that provide evidence that students have met state and local learning standards in several subject areas are important when teachers wish to promote and maintain student motivation and voice. For the standards portfolio, teachers expect students to select products of performances, projects, and other assigned work that will demonstrate the achievement levels at which students have met the standards. A language arts standards portfolio, for example, might be divided into these standards:

1. Students will read with understanding and fluency.

2. Students will write to communicate for a variety of purposes.

3. Students will listen and speak effectively in a variety of situations. (See Example 1.5 at the end of this chapter.)

When students have been informed about the purposes of standards portfolios or e-portfolios, they will want to include items that provide evidence of how they have met or exceeded the standards. The selected pieces can be accompanied with a checklist or scoring guide, also known as a "rubric," to indicate the quality of students' work and the areas in which they need to improve in order to meet or exceed the standards. On culmination of the year or semester in which the portfolio is developed, students will use the portfolio to assert their evidence of successfully meeting standards. Meanwhile, teachers using standards portfolios of their students' academic progress have authentic evidence with which they can build the case for student promotion, recognition, or award. Similarly, they have clear and compelling evidence demonstrating the successful outcomes of their teaching.

Significant Achievement or Best Work Portfolio

The significant achievement or best work portfolio is useful at both the elementary and secondary school levels. It will include items that may or may not have been graded previously, but that will be selected by the students as representative of their best achievement in the knowledge base, learning process, or competency. Student choice and voice are important components of this type of portfolio or e-portfolios. Once the teacher and the students select key items, they review the work and discover students' individual character and achievement in areas that may not be assessed on teacher-made or standardized tests. This type of portfolio highlights and acknowledges students' strengths and talents and helps bolster their sense of self-esteem and self-worth. (See Example 1.7 and Blackline 1.4 at the end of this chapter.)

Academic Content Portfolio

Educators teaching a single-subject area such as mathematics, science, language arts, art, music, or vocational education require students to demonstrate their knowledge within that content area. For example, language arts teachers may ask students to include one example of each of the following in their content portfolios: narrative essay, expository essay, and persuasive essay, poem, letter, research paper, and book report. The teacher may require that one persuasive essay be included in the portfolio, but the student chooses which persuasive essay to include.

Integrated Portfolio

The integrated portfolio encourages students, teachers, and parents to view the whole student by seeing a body of work that represents all the disciplines. The purpose of the integrated portfolio is to show the connections between or among all the subjects taught (Cole, Ryan, Kick, & Mathies, 2000). For this portfolio or e-portfolio, students select key items from several or all of their subjects. They discuss the concepts or skills that are found across several subject areas, which may even connect with ideas and achievements outside of school. The integrated portfolio works well in elementary and special education classrooms where teachers work on topic units, such as "plant life." Students include readings, mathematics problems, science projects, artwork, and music pieces, all of which are related to plant life.

Integrated portfolios for junior high or middle schools work best when a team of teachers plans the curriculum together. The team selects a theme, such as "conflict" or "social justice in America." Students include their responses to the theme based on literature from English, data and statistics from mathematics, issues of experimentation from science, and art and music projects from those classes. The integrated portfolio brings coherence and connectedness to all the disciplines for the students because it promotes a more holistic or integrated learning experience. (See Examples 1.8 and 1.9 and Blackline 1.5 at the end of this chapter.)

Cooperative Group Portfolio

Cooperative learning continues to be employed by teachers as a highly effective tool for promoting success for all students, while promoting the acquisition of needed social skills, habits of mind, and conflict-resolution skills. When led correctly, each member of the cooperative group acquires a high degree of subject-area knowledge as well as an increased ability to think critically and empathetically. When teachers elect to design cooperative group portfolios, they wish to provide evidence of the individual strengths and team skills that contribute to successful achievement for all. In this portfolio, cooperative groups select items that they can "showcase" as evidence of their group's successful performance and achievement. Group items, samples, or pictures of group projects, performance rubrics, reflections on team-building activities, and contributions to school or community projects are just some of the artifacts that demonstrate the power of the cooperative group portfolio. Individual students develop voice in the cooperative group portfolio process: Even the most reticent students often obtain a comfort level in a smaller group. They participate with their peers in reviewing criteria for artifact selection that will guide them in their joint work and self-assessment. Group portfolios may be used for conferences with other groups, teachers, and parents, as well as for showcases with the larger school community. A cooperative group portfolio emphasizes the development of various strengths and talents that students bring to the group, and fosters the ability to form positive collaborative relationships.

Multiyear (Cumulative) Portfolio

Some schools cluster grade levels together in two-, three-, or four-year intervals and require students to save specific portfolio pieces from each year. For example, students might save selected portfolio items from kindergarten, first, and second grade in different-colored folders. The folder for each grade level can be placed in an accordion folder or similar container and stored at the school. Periodically, students are invited to look over their work, reflect on their progress, and note their improvements. They might review their artwork, scientific inquiries, problem-solving activities, handwriting, cassette recordings of themselves reading, and so on. They may ask their peers or parents to review their work and offer feedback. These multiyear portfolios also chronicle students' progress toward mastering standards. Since students develop skills and abilities at different times in their development, teachers can track their progress and differentiate the curriculum to meet the individual learning needs of each student. (See Example 1.10 and Blackline 1.7 at the end of this chapter.)

SCHOOLWIDE PORTFOLIOS

Schoolwide Profile Portfolio

When schools or entire school districts wish to inform parents, community members, and others about the important learning and events that occur in the lives of the students, teachers, and school staff, the schoolwide profile portfolio is appropriate (Figure 1.5). Because it lends itself best to the e-portfolio format that is increasingly being used in many states, it is possible for teachers to lead entire classes in the selection of artifacts of joint learning or project work that they assert as being representative of their learning communities. The final multimedia product of this e-portfolio can contain (1) photofolios—class pictures with their mottoes, pictures of performances, and academic schoolwide events; (2) audios of various students describing the artifacts as they are presented; and (3) brief video clips of the classes or entire school engaged in important learning or community service activities. A portfolio design committee is often responsible for developing the purpose and process of this portfolio (Figure 1.6). This portfolio can chronicle the school year through student selection of entries, which can include events such as campus beautification day, field day, school Olympics, or international days. In addition, the schoolwide portfolio can showcase National Merit Scholarship winners, student or teacher awards, science fair projects, or musical performances.

The reflective character of the schoolwide portfolio can be inclusive by inviting all students, teachers, parents, staff, and administrators to contribute their recollections and reflections on each of the artifacts that are selected for inclusion. If completed in a traditional paper format, the school portfolio is kept in the school office or media center. The multimedia e-portfolio, however, provides an excellent platform for the schoolwide profile portfolio's inclusion on the school or school district's Web site. This site invites the public to review and learn about the varied nature of the school and the achievements of its students, faculty, and staff. This portfolio can also be used as a document in a schoolwide review, strategic plan, or accreditation study (Bernhardt, 1994).

Class Profile Portfolio

When each class within a school compiles items that can chronicle its accomplishments and provide a portrait of the class, a class profile portfolio is

---

Establish Portfolio Purpose

What is the major purpose for the portfolio?

Who will be needed to plan the portfolio around this purpose?

How will the portfolio be used?

Who will have access to the portfolio during the process?

Who will have access to the portfolio after the process?

Figure 1.5

Typical Contents of the Schoolwide Portfolio

- Pictures or videos of sporting events

- Special speakers at assemblies

- Schoolwide awards

- Field trips

- Lists of students on honor rolls

- Autographed playbills from school plays

- Events from PTA/PTO nights

Figure 1.6

created. Typical items in this portfolio or multimedia e-portfolio may include any or all of the following:

- noteworthy achievements by the class (academic or other)
- class picture, motto, or song
- class predictions
- "last wills and testaments" for the next class
- pictures or videos of class or community projects or performances
- pictures or videos of field trips, assemblies, or guest speakers
- letters from parents, administrators, congressional representatives, business leaders, or sports or movie personalities

The class portfolio can include group projects or examples of team-building activities that helped bond the class together. To provide a comprehensive portrait, portfolio designers may choose to include class poems, stories, biographical information, profiles, individual class member accomplishments celebrated by the class, short- or long-term goals, student career choices, or a collage of famous people in the news that the class has studied.

Districtwide Profile Portfolio

Districts may keep a cumulative portfolio that includes contributions from each of the schools, as well as districtwide events. Some events to include in a districtwide portfolio are

- community projects,
- scores on standardized tests,
- scholarship winners,
- schools of excellence,
- physical fitness awards,
- state or federal grants,

- computer innovations, and
- awards that students, teachers, and administrators have earned.

The districtwide portfolio provides documentation to show how the district meets accreditation requirements or standards. This type of portfolio reveals the district's strengths and weaknesses and is instrumental in planning future instructional goals. These portfolios might contain analyses of test scores, absentee rates, graduation rates, and progress toward meeting school improvement goals. This portfolio can be periodically shared with the parents, the school board, or the larger community to help guide strategic planning efforts. Some districts make this portfolio public by linking it to their Web page.

Examples

Middle School Student Portfolio Entry

Student Goal-Setting Questions		
Subject: Mathematics		
Date: March 12, 2005 Student Name <u>Anson W.</u>		

	Not Yet	*Got It*
Am I meeting stated criteria?		XX
Am I meeting my personal goals?	XX	

How should I self-inspect?
My goal in math this term was to take more time to check for accuracy in problems I complete for homework. I have improved in doing this on homework. I still need to slow down when I take quizzes and tests.
How will I know when I am on track?
Easy. I will get more points on my quizzes and tests when I find errors before I turn them in.

Example 1.1

Multiple Intelligence Portfolio: Space

Standards:

1. Use reading, writing, listening, and speaking skills to research and apply information for specific purposes.

2. Understand the facts and unifying concepts of earth/space sciences.

3. Identify and explain ways that science and technology influence the direction of people's lives.

Verbal/Linguistic	Logical/Mathematical	Visual/Spatial	Bodily/Kinesthetic
• Develop a list of vocabulary words for space. • Write a joke book for space creatures. • Write a short story set on a planet. • Keep a diary about a trip you took in space. • Research a planet.	• Graph the distances of planets from the sun or other planets. • Calculate the length of a trip to the moon traveling at 100 miles per hour. • Classify planets by temperature and size. • Calculate the cost of fuel needed to reach the moon.	• Draw a picture of what you think a Martian looks like. • Make a model of the solar system. • Make a clay sculpture of a planet. • Create a Venn diagram comparing Earth and Mars.	• Act out the astronauts' first steps on the moon. • Simulate the sun or the orbits of all the planets. • Create a sport that would be popular in space (with no gravity). • Demonstrate gravity in an experiment.
Musical/Rhythmic	Interpersonal	Intrapersonal	Naturalist
• Write a planetary anthem for one of the planets. • Write a rap song for one of the planets. • Create a new dance named *Space Walk*. • Write poetry to the music from *2001: A Space Odyssey*.	• Interview E.T. about his trip to Earth. • Role-play the parts of each member of as space crew. • Plan a joint space expedition with another country. • Practice peer mediation with an alien. • Give a speech persuading others to explore space.	• Meditate on being the first person to walk on the moon. • Describe how it would feel to be the first student in space. • Tell how you would feel if you did not see sunlight for a long time. • Write a letter to an astronaut.	• Classify plants found in space. • Identify rock samples found on planets. • Forecast the weather for a planet. • Plan a nature week on a planet. • Create a survival guide for life on Mars.

Standards Pieces	**Item 1** *Research report on planet*	**Item 2** *Speech on space exploration*	**Item 3** *Survival guide*	**Item 4** *Gravity experiment*
Student's Choice	**Item 5**	**Item 6**	**Item 7**	**Item 8**

Example 1.2

Multiple Intelligence Portfolio: Greek Mythology

Standards:

1. Communicate in writing to describe, inform, persuade, and entertain.

2. Demonstrate comprehension of a broad range of reading materials.

3. Use reading, writing, listening, and speaking skills to research and apply information for specific purposes.

Verbal/Linguistic	Logical/Mathematical	Visual/Spatial	Bodily/Kinesthetic
• Read *The Iliad*. • Read *The Odyssey*. • Read Edith Hamilton's *Mythology*. • Write an original myth to explain a scientific mystery. • Write poems about mythology. • Write a eulogy for a fallen Greek or Trojan warrior.	• Use a Venn diagram to compare the Greeks and the Trojans. • Create original story problems that can incorporate the Pythagorean theorem. • Draw a family tree of the twelve Olympians. • Complete a time line of Odysseus' trip home from Troy.	• Draw the battle plan for the Greeks' attack on Troy. • Draw Mt. Olympus. • Sketch the Greek gods and goddesses. • Create a video of the Olympic games. • Draw items that relate to mythology.	• Act out a Greek tragedy. • Re-create some of the Olympic events. • Act out a myth. • Create a dance for the forest nymphs. • Reenact the battle scene between Hector and Achilles.
Musical/Rhythmic	Interpersonal	Intrapersonal	Naturalist
• Write a song for a lyre. • Pretend you are Apollo, god of music, and CEO of Motown. • Select music that correlates to each god or goddess.	• Interview Helen about her role in the Trojan War. • Work in a group to create a digital crossword puzzle about mythology.	• Pretend you are a Greek soldier away from home for ten years. Keep a diary of your thoughts. • Write a journal about how you would feel if you were Prometheus chained to a rock.	• Using scientific data predict how long it will take before anything grows after the Greeks destroy Troy and sow the fields with salt. • Describe the animals and plants on Mt. Olympus.

Standards Pieces	Item 1	Item 2	Item 3	Item 4
	Research report on Trojan War	Persuasive essay supporting Greeks' strategies	Book report on *The Odyssey*	Original poem on mythology

Student Choice	Item 5	Item 6	Item 7	Item 8

Example 1.3

High School Student's Autobiographical Portfolio

Type of Portfolio: Personal—Autobiographical

Criteria of Portfolio	Not Yet 0	Some Evidence 1
Structure/Organization		
• Does your portfolio have a Letter to the Reader?		x
• Does your portfolio describe at least five things about you?	x	
• Does your portfolio have a closing statement?	x	
Content		
• Does your portfolio include photographs?		x
• Does your portfolio include reflective tags for each item included?	x	
• Does your portfolio have a separate section about you, your family and friends?	x	
• Does your portfolio have a section about your goals after high school?		x
Mechanics		
• Are all your sentences complete?		x
• Did you check your punctuation?		x
• Did you check all sentences for subject-verb agreement?		x

Example 1.4

Standards Portfolio Artifact for Middle School

Objective: Students will listen, speak, read, and write for information, understanding, and social interaction.

Standards:

1. Compose well-organized and coherent writing for a specific purpose and audience. Speak effectively, using appropriate language.
2. Use correct grammar, spelling, punctuation, capitalization, and sentence structure.

Task:

Your class has been selected to create an orientation program for students new to our school. The program should include a welcome letter, a tour of the school, and an information booklet about the school's history. Be prepared to present your entire program to the administration on September 28.

Group One	Group Two	Group Three
Create a welcome letter for your audience. Use correct style, grammar, and punctuation.	Design a plan and script for a tour of the school. Use correct spelling, grammar, and punctuation.	Create an information booklet about the school's history. Use correct spelling, grammar, and punctuation.

Example 1.5

Portphotos: Using Snapshots for Portfolio Assessment

April 24

Prompt: Pictures of Significance

Think of a photograph that represents a moment of significance in your life. If the photo existed, what would it show? What would this photo tell us about you? What were you doing? How does this photo help you recall that special moment in your life? How have you changed since that photo was taken?

Write a descriptive narrative about your photo. Be prepared to share your writing with your neighbor.

Example 1.6

Best Work Portfolio

Subject: American Literature

1. Annotated bibliography of writers associated with the Harlem Renaissance

2. Video clip of debate on which contemporary author deserves the Nobel Prize for Literature

3. A Venn diagram comparing Edgar Allan Poe's work with Stephen King's work

4. A critique of Hemingway's novel, *The Sun Also Rises*

5. My Top Ten List of the best American women writers (and a rationale for their ranking)

Example 1.7

Integrated Portfolio

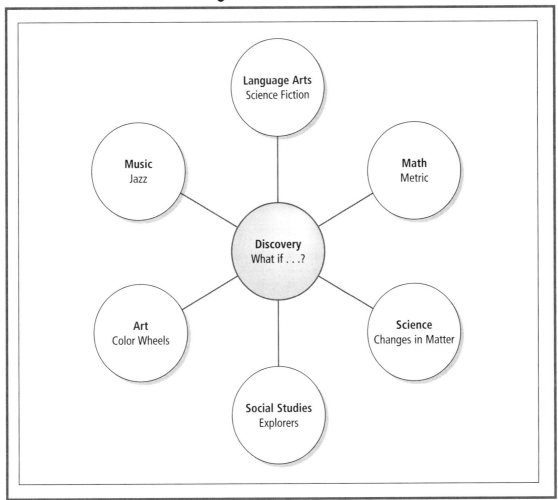

Example 1.8

Integrated Portfolio

Integrates: language arts, social studies, mathematics, science, art

Theme: Criminal Justice

1. Videotape of mock trial of Boo Radley (from *To Kill a Mockingbird*)

2. Analysis of types of capital punishment from a medical perspective

3. Graphs of the number of prisoners on death row in each state, including their race, age, and level of education

4. Journal entry on one day in the life of a death-row prisoner

5. Sketches of scenes from a courtroom or prison

6. Time lines of famous trials in American history

Example 1.9

Multiyear Portfolio

(Grades K–2)

1. Recording of student readings from each grade level

2. Two drawings from each grade level, print or digitally scanned

3. Two samples of written work from each grade level (one from the beginning of the year, one from the end of the year)

4. A video clip of one oral presentation from each year.

5. A student-selected "best work" from each year

Example 1.10

Blacklines

Portfolio Planner 1

Getting Started

Purpose

What is the *principal* purpose for using an academic portfolio?

_____

_____

What is a *secondary* purpose for using an academic portfolio?

_____

_____

Type

What type(s) of portfolios will help fulfill the purpose? Explain why.

_____

_____

_____

_____

Audience

Who will be the audience of the portfolio?

_____

_____

_____

Format

Will this be a paper portfolio or electronic portfolio (e-portfolio)?

☐ Paper   ☐ E-portfolio

Blackline 1.1

Portfolio Planner 2

Introducing Students to the Portfolio

How and when will students be introduced to the portfolio or e-portfolio?

_____
_____
_____
_____

Organizational Flow

What is the timeline for students to collect, select, reflect, and confer on the academic portfolio?

_____
_____
_____
_____

Contents

What are anticipated to be the major contents of student work in the portfolio or e-portfolio?

_____
_____
_____
_____

Organizational Tools

What types of tools (table of contents, tabs, index) will be needed to organize the portfolio or e-portfolio?

_____
_____
_____

Assessment Tools

What types of assessment tools and strategies must be introduced and taught to students?

    Before portfolio process begins

_____
_____
_____

Portfolio Planner 2 (Continued)

During portfolio process

_____

_____

_____

At the conclusion of the portfolio process

_____

_____

_____

Portfolio Storage

Where will students store their "working folders" for the portfolio?

_____

_____

Where will students store their paper portfolios?

_____

_____

How and where will students store their e-portfolios?

_____

_____

Security

How will the confidentiality of the portfolios or e-portfolios be ensured?

_____

_____

Blackline 1.2

Portfolio Planner 3

Selecting Key Artifacts

Portfolio Purpose

- Learning process
- Developmental
- Assessment/Standards
- Showcase/Best work

Portfolio Type

- Personal
- Academic
- Schoolwide (class profile, school profile, district profile)

The What

- Contents—anticipated contents of the portfolio or e-portfolio
- Learning processes—speaking, reading, writing, problem solving, etc.
- Developmental—growth and development in social skills, thinking skills, literacy, mathematical thinking, etc.
- Assessment/Standards: State learning standards in specific subjects

_____

_____

_____

_____

- Showcase/Best work: Significant achievement in specific subjects

_____

_____

_____

_____

The How

How will the portfolio processes be explained to students?

_____

_____

(Continued)

Portfolio Planner 3 (Continued)

How will the portfolio processes be explained to parents?

_____

_____

How will portfolio assessment processes be explained to students?

_____

_____

The When

When will work be selected for inclusion in the portfolio?

• Parent conferences	Date:
• End of units	Date:
• End of quarter/End of semester	Date
• End of year	Date:
• Cumulative (year to year)	Year:

The Who

Who will participate in the assessment process and selection of artifacts?

• Students	• Parents
• Teachers	• Juries (other teachers/school administrators)
• Students' peers	• Others

Comments:

_____

_____

_____

Blackline 1.3

Planning the Showcase Portfolio

Purpose: Showcase/Best Work

Directions: Select the content areas that will be included in the showcase portfolio and list any relevant standards; list curricular objectives related to the student work to be included in the portfolio. Brainstorm on the three types of assessment that will provide the most compelling evidence of student achievement.

Content Area(s)	Standards to Be Met

Curriculum Objectives

_____

_____

Assessments for Learning

1. _____
2. _____
3. _____
4. _____

Assessments of Learning

1. _____
2. _____
3. _____
4. _____

Blackline 1.4

Integrated Portfolio

Select a theme (Courage, Rebellion, Space, Environment, the Future, etc.) and brainstorm portfolio entries for each subject area listed in the boxes below.

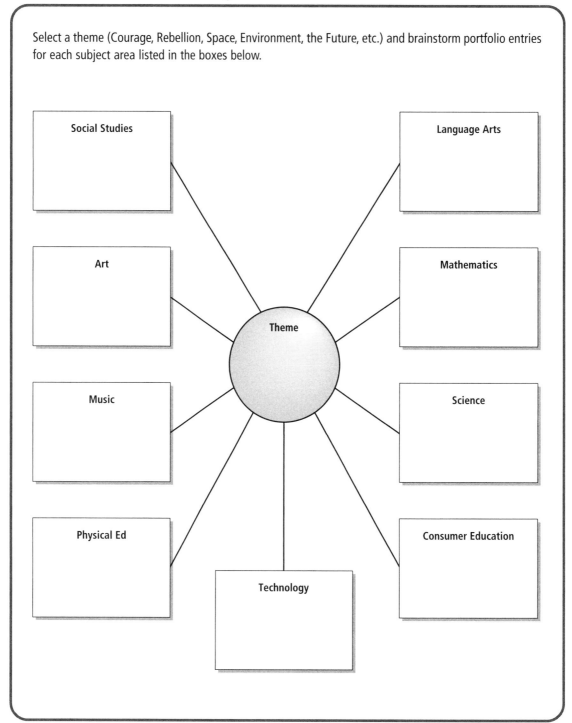

Blackline 1.5

Planning the Standards Portfolio

Purpose: Assessment/Standards

Directions: Select a content area for the standards portfolio and list the relevant standards, and then list curricular objectives. Brainstorm on the three types of assessment that will provide the most compelling evidence of student achievement.

Content Area _____

Standards to Be Met

_____

_____

_____

_____

Curriculum Objectives to Be Achieved

_____

_____

_____

_____

Assessments for Learning

1. _____
2. _____
3. _____
4. _____

Assessments of Learning

1. _____
2. _____
3. _____
4. _____

Blackline 1.6

Multiyear Portfolio

My Portfolio Can Help Me Tell My Story

Student Name _____ Date _____

1. Label your work according to the grade level.
2. Spread out the work by dates (earliest date to most current date).
3. Select three writing assignments (one from each year).
4. Line them up in order and review them carefully.
5. Answer the following questions about your three samples:

What major difference do you see?

_____

_____

What surprised you the most?

_____

_____

How have your interests changed?

_____

_____

What skills (handwriting, grammar, spelling, organization, vocabulary, etc.) do you still need to develop more? Why?

_____

_____

6. Show your three sample pieces to a peer. Ask for comments about any changes he or she sees.

   Peer Comments: _____

7. Set new goals for yourself.

   Goal One: _____

   Goal Two: _____

   Goal Three: _____

Blackline 1.7

Planning the Developmental Portfolio

Purpose: Developmental

Directions: Select the developmental process for the portfolio and list the relevant benchmarks. Brainstorm on the types of assessment that will provide evidence of student development over time.

Development Process _____

Benchmarks That Will Determine Progress:

_____

_____

_____

_____

Assessments for Learning

1. _____

2. _____

3. _____

4. _____

Assessments of Learning

1. _____

2. _____

3. _____

4. _____

Blackline 1.8

Planning the Learning Process Portfolio

Purpose: Learning Process

Directions: Select the learning process and content for the portfolio and list the relevant benchmarks. Brainstorm on the types of assessment that will provide evidence of student development over time.

Learning Process _____

Benchmarks That Will Determine Progress:

_____

_____

_____

_____

Assessments for Learning

1. _____

2. _____

3. _____

4. _____

Assessments of Learning

1. _____

2. _____

3. _____

4. _____

Blackline 1.9

Multiple Intelligences Portfolio

Unit: _____ Time Frame: _____ Grade/Subject: _____

Standards: 1. _____

2. _____

3. _____

Verbal/Linguistic	Logical/Mathematical	Visual/Spatial	Bodily/Kinesthetic
Musical/Rhythmic	Interpersonal	Intrapersonal	Naturalist

	Item 1	Item 2	Item 3	Item 4
Standards Pieces				

	Item 5	Item 6	Item 7	Item 8
Student Choice				

Blackline 1.10

2

Connect Portfolio Design to Developmental Stages

OVERVIEW

This chapter will present the ways that an academic portfolio can work for you and your students. You will learn how to consider the different ages and stages of learners in order to design the portfolio around these characteristics. We will explore many ways to make the portfolio work, including how to get started and how to select tools from the many palettes of portfolio processes. The chapter will also discuss how to adapt the e-portfolio to students' technology levels, from emergent to proficient.

You will learn how to design a developmentally appropriate process that aligns with the different ages and stages of your student learners. You will learn where to start and how you can adapt the portfolio to students' individual learning needs as you proceed through the portfolio's design and implementation.

INTRODUCTION

As the portfolio and e-portfolio have been used in different states as well as many countries around the world, it has become increasingly clear that the design of the portfolio needs to be a good "fit" with the learners. Just as good

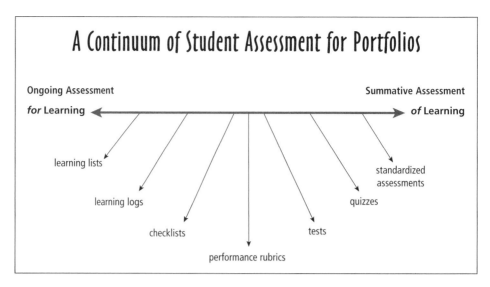

Figure 2.1

curriculum and instruction begin with consideration of the learner, so does the portfolio design process. Effective portfolio processes are those that include and build on student "voice." They might begin with the simple practice of inviting young children to "tell me about" your writing. Later, the portfolio process succeeds by engaging students in self-assessment of known achievement criteria on projects and performances to which the teacher or parents provide informal feedback. This is then extended by promoting student engagement in ongoing decision making on the collection and selection stages of their portfolios. In essence, the decision to promote student voice in portfolios helps teachers and portfolio designers to use assessment for learning (Stefanakis, 2002; see also Figure 2.1).

Portfolios then become a "process of seeking and interpreting evidence for use by learners and their teachers to decide where the learners are in their learning, where they need to go and how best to get there" (Barrett, 2004b).

DEVELOPMENTAL STAGES AND LEARNING NEEDS

Preprimary

With preprimary aged children four to five, the portfolio process might be one of continuous reflection, interview, and dictation. Teachers of young children know that they can be introduced to simple portfolios of significant achievement with relative ease. In Western Australia, for example, many teachers use portfolios as a means by which they collect samples of children's work. Used in kindergartens in Australia, a portfolio can be a scrapbook, folder, or any container in which a child's work is placed for viewing by parents, teachers, and others. Parents agree that their youngsters love to share pieces of their art or early schoolwork that they enjoyed creating. As every parent knows, young children eagerly share the fruits of their play and work, whether it has occurred in the block corner, on the writing table, or at the science center. By using very simple portfolio tools, teachers can initiate a process whereby children attach meaning to their work and to participate in an ongoing organization process that results in a portfolio that the children can share with parents and significant others. For example, one teacher uses "descriptors" for every piece of work that will ultimately be selected for the preprimary child's portfolio. In addition to promoting clear understanding of the curricular organization for the teacher, descriptors, as parents say they have found, are useful for understanding the activity. Parents like to see where their child excels and what skills their child still needs to work on (Cox, 2007). Figure 2.2 illustrates a way in which descriptors (results) promote clarity for all participants of the preprimary portfolio.

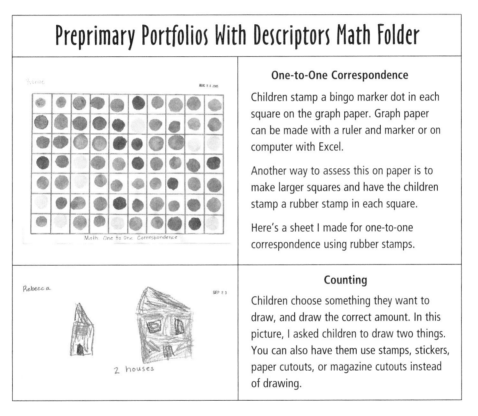

Preprimary Portfolios With Descriptors Math Folder

One-to-One Correspondence

Children stamp a bingo marker dot in each square on the graph paper. Graph paper can be made with a ruler and marker or on computer with Excel.

Another way to assess this on paper is to make larger squares and have the children stamp a rubber stamp in each square.

Here's a sheet I made for one-to-one correspondence using rubber stamps.

Counting

Children choose something they want to draw, and draw the correct amount. In this picture, I asked children to draw two things. You can also have them use stamps, stickers, paper cutouts, or magazine cutouts instead of drawing.

Figure 2.2

SOURCE: www.prekinders.com/front2.jpg. Used with permission from Karen Cox.

Preprimary portfolio processes clearly acknowledge children's unfolding gifts and predispositions in a variety of learning areas. They also provide a platform on which children's pride in their work and (play) can grow throughout their continuing school years. To get young children started with a portfolio, it is suggested that teachers focus on the children's central role in the portfolio process.

(1) Show children what a portfolio is and explain how they will use one in class. (2) Discuss how older students use portfolios for job interviews and college entrances. Explain how some adults use portfolios for job advancement or to obtain a new job. When possible, invite older students or adults to share their portfolios with the children and explain why portfolios are important and useful in their lives. (3) Discuss the children's ownership and pride. Explain how they will be responsible for filing and organizing their work, just as adults do in their jobs. (Kingore, 2008, pp. 18–19).

The most appropriate tools for promoting this kind of involvement of preprimary children are the learning logs, learning lists, individual checklists, small-group checklists, and, in some cases, journals. Teachers and parents initially serve as "facilitators" who spread out the dated "artifacts" of student work on a table and lead them into conversation about which pieces they like best. Parents often do this with the school- or home-created works that end up on the refrigerator door! (See Example 2.1 at the end of this chapter.)

Primary

Determining how to involve primary-aged children in portfolios is similar to determining how to involve preprimary stage children, but also including children's evolving literacy as a value-added aspect. Here, children are increasingly able to complete their own learning lists, learning logs, and journals. They are developing the ability to participate in determining the criteria for the completion of narratives, performances, and individual and group projects. They are also able to use emergent and conventional literacy to create *tags* for their paper portfolios and graphics and hyperlinks for their e-portfolios. An example of an early primary student's reflection on an assessment tool is shown in Figure 2.3. (See Examples 2.2, 2.3, and 2.4 and Blackline 2.1 at the end of this chapter.)

Early Primary Student Reflection

Name: Sean   Date: January 28

My Portfolio: Math

I know what the + sign means.

I know what the − sign means.

I can show my work with teddy bear counters.

Figure 2.3

Intermediate—Middle School

Assessment practices become more high-stakes for students as they move from the self-contained classroom of the elementary school into the middle school or junior high school. At this level, where subject-area knowledge is delivered to students in roughly 50-minute classes taught by different teachers, the challenge is to maintain a lens on the student rather than on the subject area. With a range of 100 to 150 students or more, it is often difficult for a teacher to see the student as a whole person rather than as a "math" student, "language arts" student, or "science" student. This is why the use of academic portfolios containing student-selected artifacts of content or learning processes that are evaluated with authentic assessments is especially critical. When educators apply their knowledge of child development to the design of curriculum, instruction, and assessment, they are more likely to provide classroom-learning environments in which students develop voice, motivation, and the determination to succeed. They promote continuing social and cognitive development through teaching and learning events that help students to understand the connections between what is learned in one class and what is learned in others. With this in mind, the National Middle School Association (2006) has noted that

> We must create opportunities for students to connect and make sense of the pieces of their learning as well. Students must have opportunities to use their skills and knowledge to demonstrate their understanding of issues and ideas. Multiple assessment strategies are needed to validate the multiple ways students make sense of their learning. Students need time to reflect on the work they do and to make the connections between and among tasks. This personal understanding, this personal integration of knowledge, is at the heart of the best assessment practices. (p. 2)

The portfolio and e-portfolio process fosters student development in a wider variety of cognitive and social areas. It encourages individual students to apply developing cognitive skills of reflection and metacognition and promotes their ability to analyze thinking processes, dispositions, and feelings about themselves as individual learners or team members. Portfolio processes offer them opportunities to self-assess progress on difficult skills or concepts, as well as opportunities to apply new knowledge in the larger context. They also give them the opportunity to see adults as caring people with whom they can communicate about the successes and difficulties that they experience as they study and learn in each of their middle school or junior high courses. Examples of middle school students' reflection and assessment tools can be found in Figures 2.4 and 2.5. (See Blackline 2.2 at the end of this chapter.)

This alignment of academic portfolio processes with developmental capabilities is vital to the teacher's success in introducing and maintaining effective portfolio and e-portfolio processes with middle school and junior high school students.

High School

Secondary school educators agree that by the time most students arrive at high school, they have become accustomed to assessment as something that is *done to* them rather than a process in which they participate in a meaningful manner. Some research has validated that the student "turn-off syndrome" is often accentuated because students find that their work is judged by someone else using criteria that are meaningless to them.

Beyond "percent correct," assigned letter grades, and grammatical or arithmetic errors, many students have little knowledge of what is involved in evaluating their work. Portfolios can provide structure for involving students in developing and understanding criteria for good efforts, in coming to see the criteria as their own, and in applying the criteria to their own and other students' work. (Sweet, 1993, p. 1)

Middle School Student Reflection

Name: Abigail   Date: October 17

I earned a B on this project.

I know this because I reached the benchmark on every part of the rubric. I also know that I learned a lot from doing the model of the solar system.

I am putting it in my working portfolio because it shows that I know how to follow directions, use a rubric, and work hard to make a good model.

Figure 2.4

Middle School Student Assessment

Name: Abigail   Date: October 17

	Not Yet	*Almost there*	*Got it*
Label all the planets	Did not label any planets	Labeled half the planets	Labeled all the planets
Use resources	Used only one resource	Used three resources	Used five resources
Use correct spelling	Misspelled all planet names	Spelled all planet names correctly	Spelled all planet names correctly

Figure 2.5

Portfolios and e-portfolios have been used for many years at the high school level. At places like the famed Central Park East Secondary School in Manhattan, Deborah Meier and other progressive educators began to experiment with judging low-income inner-city students on the basis of collections of their best work and oral examinations. They found that if students did well on these alternative assessments, they gained admission to college and tended to do well there. Vermont educator Carol Smith, who advanced the use of portfolios in that state (2004), asserts that "students hold important information about what they know and what they are able to do, as well as what they don't know and are unable to do. Given the opportunity, students can competently discuss their learning and their growth with others" (p. 1). Portfolios and e-portfolios provide just this kind of opportunity for students from the first day of classes through the culmination of their studies. An example of secondary students' use of assessment tools to reflect is shown in Figure 2.6.

PORTFOLIOS AND CURRICULUM ALIGNMENT

An important benefit of the portfolio or e-portfolio planning process is the way in which the inclusion of student voice in assignments and authentic assessments results in more successful curriculum alignment. While designing the purposes and procedures of the portfolio, teachers consider four main questions (Figure 2.7) that were stressed by educator Tyler (1969). (See Blackline 2.5 at the end of this chapter.)

High School Rubric on Student Performance on a Team Project

Evaluating Myself	1	2	3
Motivation	I didn't try my best	I tried to do better	(I did my best work)
Work	I didn't do a lot	(I did a good amount of work)	I did all of the expected work and went above and beyond
Contribution	I didn't help a lot	I aided in some aspects	(Our team worked well because I did my best to contribute to the group as a whole.)
Total: 9 Points			

I think I did much better with this group project. I worked hard to do my best work and tried to help my team. When we got off task, I tried to stay in my role as the checker/timekeeper.

Student Name: Martina

Figure 2.6

CONNECTING WITH E-PORTFOLIOS

Those educators who seek to create an e-portfolio process will find it equally important to assess the developmental capabilities of students in order to utilize electronic tools such as word processing and presentation software; digital cameras and scanners; Web-editing software; and even graphics software. E-portfolios have been successfully implemented in K–12 education as supplements or alternatives to high-stakes testing. The ease of use that students display in applying hypertext links is testimony to this. Students also enjoy the flexibility that e-portfolios provide, including many opportunities for them to apply technological or artistic talents. When even the youngest students are given the opportunity to create an e-portfolio, they often go beyond teachers' expectations.

Portfolio and Curriculum Alignment

To begin aligning the portfolio to the developmental learning needs of students, the following questions can be considered:

1. What purposes should the portfolio or e-portfolio attain?

   Consider the learner: What is the developmental level in literacy development, social skills, and ability to engage in reflection or metacognition?
   - Prekindergarten (Preprimary)
   - 1st–3rd grade (Primary)
   - 4th–6th grade (Intermediate)
   - 7th–8th grade (Middle or Junior High School)

   Consider the community: What is the learning climate of the classroom? Do students engage in active communication or interaction with one another, or are interactions principally teacher led?

   Consider the subject matter: Will students be developmentally capable of selecting pieces from the subject matter that they understand to be significant evidence of their accomplishments?

   Screen through belief about how learning occurs: How will the portfolio be used as a container of evidence that is aligned with a developmentally appropriate theory of how students at this level learn?

   State in terms of behavior and content: Will the portfolio be designed in such a way that it reflects the age-appropriate behaviors and learning process of the student?

2. How can the learning experiences to be reflected in the portfolio or e-portfolio be useful in attaining these purposes? The selected pieces will reflect learning experiences that are
   - Consistent with your objectives
   - Satisfying to the learners (intrinsically motivating, with a mix of individual and collaborative work and responsibility)
   - Variable (demonstrate multiple intelligences)
   - Multiple effects (reflection on these outcomes can lead to future study and thinking)

3. How can the developmentally appropriate learning experiences be organized into a portfolio or e-portfolio?
   - *Continuity:* Pieces included in the portfolio reflect student learning that has resulted from direct instruction, as well as from individual and group engagement in active or constructive learning experiences.
   - *Presence of breadth and depth:* The portfolio is designed to demonstrate student understanding and performance at various stages of content exploration or knowledge construction.
   - *Integration:* Several subject areas or skills are represented in evidence to be selected for the portfolio.

4. How can the portfolio or e-portfolio effectively demonstrate the developmentally appropriate quality of the learning experiences reflected by the artifacts?
   - *Assessment of learning dispositions, social skills, and intelligent behaviors:* The portfolio includes pieces in which students' developmental level in these areas was clearly assessed or self-assessed.
   - *Assessment of lesson effectiveness:* Opportunity to fine-tune is built into the portfolio through the development of evaluation questions (student led in upper grades) that align with the developmental learning levels of the students.
   - *Assessment of learning objectives:* Effective assessment rubrics of learning outcomes have been designed for or with students prior to selection for the portfolio.

Figure 2.7

Because students typically demonstrate rapidly developing skill in using multimedia technologies, teachers need to continually determine students' skill in using technology as both an information-seeking tool and a communication tool (e-mail, discussion boards, blogs, and synchronous chat rooms). A distinguished practitioner and researcher in the use of e-portfolios, Barrett (2006) has published a summary of the advantages and disadvantages of the most popularly used e-tools for portfolios (Figure 2.8).

We believe that the use of student e-portfolios for the same purposes as portfolios is optimal to the continued progress, motivation, and success of students in the elementary and secondary levels of schooling. More ideas about e-portfolios will be found in the following chapters.

Advantages and Disadvantages of E-tools for Portfolios

Tool	Advantages	Disadvantages
Microsoft Office (or OpenOffice.org)	Available on most personal computers, is a common toolset, and makes creating hyperlinks easy. Does not require Internet access to develop portfolios (students work off-line). Better for publishing on LAN, CD.	Requires setting up own system for storing and organizing files and managing the feedback on student work (probably using Track Changes in Word or Comments in all tools). Data aggregation must be set up with another tool, like Excel, not automated. Files should be translated into Web-compatible format before posting online (HTML or PDF).
Think.com—a free service to K–12 schools by Oracle *My Think.com Portfolio* (PDF screen shots only)	Free. School accounts only. Principal has to sign up. Integrated with Think quest resources. Protected site, teacher can manage e-mail recipients and senders. Stickies (reflective tags) to provide feedback on student Web pages.	Set up own system for managing the feedback on student work. Data aggregation must be set up by teacher with another tool, like Excel, not automated. More of a Web page.
iLife06 (Mac only) *My iWeb Portfolio*	Seamless integration of video/audio into portfolios created with iWeb (or iDVD) and iMovie, iPhoto, iTunes, and Garage Band. Use iDVD for creating DVD portfolios (video or image/slide shows). Use iWeb to publish Web-based portfolios (create offline and upload).	Cost (free on new Macintosh computers). Requires server to publish pages (or .Mac account) or DVD writer (for iDVD).
Web Page Editors *My Composer Portfolio*	Flexibility and creativity in portfolio authoring. Helps students build technology skills.	Requires Web server (unless publishing on CD). High learning curve, difficult to support all students.
Open Source Portfolios *OSP* (part of the Sakai project, *Elgg*)	Free customized system, large community of users.	Requires a server and someone to maintain it. Volunteer developers often cannot respond to enhancement requests.
Web 2.0 tools (see list and links below)	Free, often open-source tools available on the World Wide Web.	Requires higher technology competency, mostly not secure Web sites.
WikiSpaces *My WikiSpaces Portfolio*	Free (for education) online system. Allows 2 GB online storage. All URLs are automatically converted to Weblinks. Upload any type of a file, link from any page. Page can be edited by approved members. Discussion link on top of every page.	Higher learning curve. Need to manually construct navigation menu. Does not allow organizing files into folders. Archived version does not save navigation menu. No data management tool, to aggregate.

Figure 2.8

SOURCE: Barrett, 2006, p. 6.

Examples

●●●

Preprimary Development Portfolio Reflection

Rocks

Story dictation to teacher:

Rocks are hard.

Rocks are bigger than stones.

I like to look at rocks.

I know how rocks and stones are the same.

Example 2.1

Primary Developmental Portfolio Reflection

Science

What I learned from this lesson:

I learned that water has lots of forms.

Water can be a cold liquid, and then it can sweat on the glass.

And then water can be in the air; And then water can be rain from clouds.

I learned new things in this lesson.

Example 2.2

Portphoto 1

May 11

Dear Reader,
I used to only be able to write half a page, but now I can write about ten pages.
In math, I only knew how to add, subtract, and multiply. Now I can add, subtract, multiply, divide, and do fractions.
In my portfolio it has some good stuff, and some bad stuff, but at least the bad stuff was worth a try!...

Sincerely,
Steven

Example 2.3

SOURCE: Used with permission from Elaine Adelman, Intern Coordinator, California State University, Northridge.

Portphoto 2

Parent Relections

Please respond to these questions after viewing your child's portfolio. You may write your responses to these questions in the form of a letter addressed to your child.

1. What items did you find of most interest in this portfolio?

The insight about how you can improve and master new areas of learning.

2. What story, piece of writing, or activity captured your interest?

I loved the galleon story of the cook.

3. What evidence of growth do you see in this body of work?

Complete sentences, great spelling, nice handwriting.

4. What changes do you see in your child as a learner?

Open to the idea of preparation and study for examinations. Open to the use of pneumonics to memorize facts for essay writing.

5. What questions do you wish to ask your child about his/her work?

Are you challenged to learn new things?
Do you do your very best at all times?

Name: _____

Date: _5-19-_ _____

Elaine Adelman

Example 2.4

SOURCE: Used with permission from Elaine Adelman, Intern Coordinator, California State University, Northridge.

Primary Student's Writing Portfolio Reflection

Student Name: Nevar

Date: May 24, 2007

How my writing has changed: *My writing is more clear. I use capitals and I know how to put periods in.*

How I have grown as a writer: *I used to hate to write. Now I like to write because it is fun to tell a story about what I drew.*

How I have grown in my work habits: *I turn in my writing homework on time every day.*

What is special about my portfolio: *It shows how I went from not liking writing to being a good writer.*

Example 2.5

Blacklines

* * *

Early Primary Student's Reflection and Assessment Tools

Primary Student's Writing Portfolio Reflection

Student Name _____

How my writing has changed:

_____

_____

How I have grown as a writer:

_____

_____

How I have grown in my work habits:

_____

_____

What is special about my portfolio:

_____

_____

Blackline 2.1

Middle School Student's
Reflection and Assessment Tool

Name: _____   Date: _____

Criteria	No Evidence 0	Evidence 1
Research		
• 3 Types of Sources		
• 10 Notecards		
• 5 Bibliography Cards		
Organization		
• Outline (3 Roman Numerals)		
• Introduction (1 Paragraph)		
• Body (3+ Paragraphs)		
• Conclusion (1 Paragraph)		
• Bibliography (5 Sources)		
Content		
• Thesis Statement (take a stand)		
• 4–5 Pro Arguments (support stand)		
• 2–3 Con Arguments (give opposition)		
• 5 Quotes From Experts (APA form)		

Comments: _____

_____

_____

_____

_____

_____

Grade: _____

Scale:
10–12 points = A
8–9 points = B
5–7 points = C
Below 7 = Not Yet

Blackline 2.2

Planning Matrix

Learning Process Portfolio

Student: _____ Class: _____ Date: _____

Assessment Tools	Speaking	Listening	Writing	Reading	Checking for Accuracy	Problem Solving	Questioning	Using Prior Knowledge

✔ At least one artifact

\+ Two or more artifacts

− Ongoing piece

Blackline 2.3

Double-Entry Journal

Student: _____ Grade: _____

Subject: _____

Date: _____ Date: _____

Starting My Portfolio	Upon Completion of My Portfolio

Signed: _____   Signed: _____

Blackline 2.4

Portfolios and Curriculum Alignment

1. *What purposes should the portfolio or e-portfolio serve?*

This is where the developmental level in learning processes, skills, and content area are considered.

_____

_____

2. *How can the learning experiences to be reflected in the portfolio or e-portfolio be useful in serving these purposes?*

How will the pieces be satisfying to the learners, intrinsically motivating through balance of individual and collaborative work that is included?

_____

_____

How will the portfolio be variable? That is, will it include artifacts that reflect multiple ways of thinking and learning?

_____

_____

How will the portfolio promote multiple effects? That is, will the reflection on learning outcomes, products, or performances lead to future study and thinking?

_____

_____

3. *How can developmentally appropriate learning experiences be organized into a portfolio or e-portfolio?*

_____

_____

How will portfolios help promote continuity of the instructional program by including artifacts that reflect student learning that has resulted from direct instruction, as well as individual and group engagement in active or constructive learning experiences?

_____

_____

How will portfolios promote breadth and depth? That is, how will they demonstrate student understanding and performance at various stages of content exploration and knowledge construction?

_____

_____

How will portfolios promote integration? (That is, how will several subject areas or skills be represented?)

_____

_____

4. _How can the portfolio or e-portfolio effectively demonstrate the developmentally appropriate quality of the learning experiences reflected by the artifacts?_

_____

_____

How will the decision-making process consider the assessment for learning—student dispositions, social skills, and intelligent behaviors?

_____

_____

How will the portfolio include pieces in which students' developmental level in identified areas are clearly assessed or self-assessed?

_____

_____

How will the portfolio promote assessment of learning effectiveness—that is, the opportunity to fine-tune through evaluation questions students reflect on that align with their developmental learning levels?

_____

_____

How will the portfolio promote effective assessment of learning outcomes? (checklists, rubrics, etc.) designed for or along with students prior to portfolio selection.

_____

_____

Blackline 2.5

Connect Portfolio Content to Local and State Standards and Curricula

In addition to being challenged by the variability of student ability and development, teachers are often overwhelmed by the expanding and sometimes deepening curriculum. They are challenged to become effective at knowing what to teach in depth and what to cover quickly. The academic learning standards that are now found in most states and countries help teachers focus on the key knowledge, skills, and dispositions students need to know or build on for the achievement of learning. And of course, student-learning preparation is usually measured by standardized tests. Figure 3.1 lists the ways in which standards can benefit students, educators, and parents if they serve as guideposts for multidimensional learning opportunities, not mandated prescriptions for "one-size-fits-all" learning.

INTRODUCTION

Most educators have come to know curriculum standards as a set of learning expectations that have been developed by teachers, university professors, and professional organizations. State standards are often adopted through legislative bodies after they have been disseminated for review and response among educators, parents, citizens at large, and business leaders. These standards,

Standards as Guideposts

Standards can benefit students by helping educators:

S ynthesize educational goal

T arget student achievement

A lign curriculum systemically

N otify the public of results

D etermine criteria for quality work

A nalyze data

R efocus instructional methodology

D edicate resources to professional development

S erve the needs of a diverse population

Figure 3.1

SOURCE: Burke, K. (2005). *How to Assess Authentic Learning, 5th edition* (p. 13). Thousand Oaks, CA: Corwin Press.

accompanied by more detailed learning objectives called *benchmarks*, often serve to clarify the expectations in subject areas for students, while providing guidelines for teachers to assist students (and their parents) in meeting them. Many districts and states have developed content and performance standards for student learning that define what students should know and be able to do as a result of their schooling. Standards should ideally serve educators as *road maps* that help them focus on the critical areas students need to master in order to move to the next level of learning.

THE ROLE OF STANDARDS IN EDUCATION

An increased pressure for all elementary- and secondary-level students to meet standards has arisen from what has been called "the achievement gap" and subsequent U.S. federal legislation, the No Child Left Behind Act, that was discussed in the Introduction. Gergen (2005) comments that American educators clearly recognize that the two highest priorities in public schools today are to close the achievement gap and to ensure that all children, even those from the most promising backgrounds, are better prepared to meet the competitive challenges of rising nations. Kohn (1999) warns about what he describes as "five fatal flaws" of the tougher standards movement:

> (1) It gets motivation wrong. When you get [students] too focused on how well they're doing, they tend to lose interest in what they're doing. (2) It gets improvement wrong. The emphasis placed on difficulty is out of proportion to its actual significance in judging how good a classroom, school, or district is. (3) It gets teaching and learning wrong. . . . The standards' implicit assumption is that all [students] should be able to do the same things at the same rate. Any practice that requires marching in lockstep is bound to leave a lot of failures in its wake. (4) It gets assessment wrong. When districts teach to the test in order to raise test scores, this typically means worse teaching is going on. (5) It gets school reform wrong. Right now accountability is just a code word for more control over what happens in classrooms by people who are not in classrooms, and it has essentially the same effect on learning that a noose has on breathing. (p. 1)

Schlechty (2005) notes that twenty-first-century schools need to move away from the industrial-age metaphor of the bell-shaped curve: "It is no longer realistic to provide education in a manner that 'defaults' to mediocrity or failure as an acceptable level for a large number of the students they serve" (p. 3). For the same reason, those students who quickly master skills and meet standards need not endure repetitive lessons.

Teachers have the incredible challenge of differentiating instruction that will both address the needs of widely diverse student populations and meet standards. In many cases they must do so with limited means or flexibility. Students who score low on standardized tests or do not meet standards in curricular assignments as a result of such limitations often respond with frustration, embarrassment, or disruptive behaviors. Those students who master the standards quickly become bored or disengaged by what is, to them, monotonous repetition and drilling of skills they already know.

Regardless of the curricular area, teachers have found that portfolios and e-portfolios of student performance can help them accomplish a number of teaching goals that meet and extend beyond the subject area standards. These performance tasks allow teachers to create learning experiences while clustering standards and objectives. Working within the portfolio or e-portfolio processes, students become more engaged in reflecting on ways in which their work meets curricular standards. They begin to see the connections between class discussions, research, and finished products that experienced writers or researchers often take for granted. With the increased use of e-portfolios, they also become highly motivated to acquire more knowledge; they are eager to display this knowledge with the increasing number of technological communication tools available in our PreK–12 classrooms.

This is one of many reasons why performance tasks are an important part of standards-based portfolios. As they provide evidence of student achievement and teacher accountability, they become important tools in the high-stakes academic environment of today's schools. Performance tasks have the following key characteristics: (1) Students have voice in the design of the performance task; (2) the task states the curricular area and the standard to be met and makes the purpose clear to the students; (3) a rubric or similar scoring tool is created; and (4) the audience for the task is considered (specifically if outside reviewers will be involved).

Portfolios that are connected to district or state performance standards promote student success while developing students' autonomy, initiative, and voice. Standards-based portfolios engage students as active composers of academic evidence that provides information about how the standards have been addressed, met, or exceeded by students.

Portfolios and e-portfolios have become recognized as user-friendly solutions to meeting the varied responsibilities of teachers and the needs of the students they serve. While it is no small task, many educators find that bringing together these seemingly disparate considerations (the needs of students and the demands of curriculum) within the portfolio process can result in success for all. As teachers who engage in the portfolio process develop an active working knowledge of student learning standards, they seek out colleagues in order to construct meaningful and authentic tasks that can result in convincing evidence of student achievement. When developing portfolio purposes and procedures that result in standards-based student evidence, teachers find that they have begun to study the developmental levels of their students and how they can best achieve and show evidence of meeting state learning standards.

Promising evidence of this is seen at the CHIME Institute Charter Schools in California, which serve children with special needs in regular education classrooms. (See their Web site at www.chimeinstitute.org/.) The faculty has turned to portfolios as a means to provide authentic assessment for every student. Using standards asserted by the state of California, developmental and showcase portfolios, as well as student-led portfolio conferences, are implemented throughout the year as teachers and students collect and show evidence of subject area achievement.

Many high schools have found that students' digital portfolios can be important ways to provide several important aspects of their learning achievement to their teachers, administrators, parents, and others. Figure 3.2 provides a "screen shot" from a student digital e-portfolio. This example clearly demonstrates the way in which standards come alive as evidence of student achievement in the e-portfolio.

First, the description of the standard is presented. Second, the scoring rubric or criteria that were used to achieve and score the artifact are shown. Third, the artifact itself is presented along with the fourth aspect, a reflective statement from the student that expresses a rationale as to why this piece met or exceeded the standard. (This is often accompanied by an audio or video clip made by the students.)

The paper portfolio can similarly provide evidence of student achievement of standards. The standard is clearly stated the artifact is clearly presented with highlights as to the evidence of achievement, and the student includes a reflective statement that provides the viewer with a rationale as to why this piece was selected from among many others to show "what," "how," and "why" the standard was met or exceeded. Figure 3.3 provides a sample artifact from an elementary student's e-portfolio.

Middle School Student's Self-Assessment of Earthquake Rubric

STUDENTS WILL MEET THE FOLLOWING HIGH SCHOOL STANDARDS:

1. Participate in scientific inquiry and construct logical conclusions based on evidence.

2. Understand critical aspects of the flow of matter and energy within the geosphere.

3. Investigate the results of the motions of plates, including volcanoes, earthquakes, mountain building, and other geologic activities.

Rubric for Group Presentation

Group Name: *The Plate Tectonics*

Criteria	Not Yet 1	Almost There 2	Got It! 3
Did the student participate cooperatively in the group?	Evidence of many problems with cooperation in the group	Some problems that were overcome in the cooperative group.	The group showed strong evidence of cooperation and achievement.
Did the student clearly explain his or her points?	Points were unclear or difficult to understand.	Student clearly explained some of the points.	Student clearly explained all points.
Did the student speak for the same amount of time as other group members?	Amount of time for each presentation was unevenly distributed.	Speaking time for each student was somewhat even.	Speaking time for each student was distributed equally.
Did the group follow instructions? Did its research and report answer all the required questions?	The group showed evidence of confusion with instructions; minimal evidence of research in reporting answers to questions.	Directions were followed well. Required questions were answered satisfactorily with evidence of research.	Directions were followed well. Answers to required questions were excellent with strong evidence of research.
Were the group's overall conclusions logical and based on sound research?	Conclusions did not provide convincing evidence of sound research.	Evidence of sound research in group's overall conclusions.	Strong evidence of sound research in logical conclusions made by the group
TOTAL SCORE: 13	A = 13–15; B = 10–12; C = 7–10; D = 5–6; F = 0–5		

Figure 3.2

E-portfolio Artifact

"Whole Lot of Shaking Going On"

This is our group's display of our presentation about the California earthquakes.

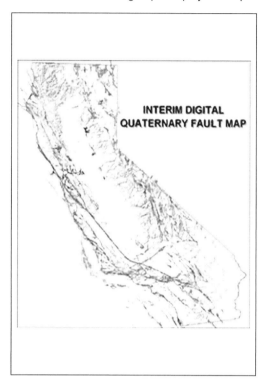

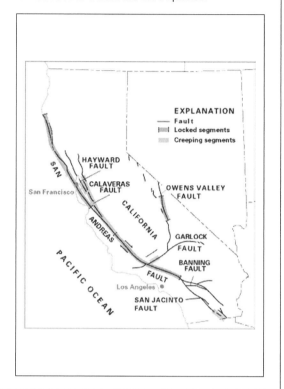

SOURCE: U.S. Geological Survey and California Geological Survey. (2006). *Quaternary fault and fold database for the United States.* Retrieved January 9, 2006, from http://earthquake.usgs.gov/regional/qfaults/faq.php. Used with permission.

Artifact Reflection for Science E-portfolio

We worked well together as a group once we understood how we were going to get the information. We had some disagreements, but we worked them out. We found good information in our books and classroom maps, but the best information we found was on the Internet.

Our group divided the work evenly, and each one of us had the same amount of time to present the answers to the questions.

We think our audience agreed with our conclusions that everyone living in an earthquake fault area should be prepared for one to happen.

Figure 3.3

PORTFOLIOS HELP STUDENTS INTEGRATE FINE ARTS

When teachers seek to include the fine arts into the curriculum, portfolios and e-portfolios are effective in providing students with opportunities to show their talents while making connections with various subject areas. For example, many teachers who seek to keep fine arts as an important curricular area in their schools create assignments that integrate the fine arts into language arts, social studies, and science standards. While the paper portfolio is an excellent vehicle for achieving this, the e-portfolio excels in promoting the integration of knowledge and skills derived from assignments across the subject areas. The following example details how secondary school and junior high students studying scientific discovery can link concepts to language arts themes and discuss new knowledge with a variety of language arts conventions.

By applying the purposes and procedures of portfolios toward the achievement of academic standards, educators can better ensure that students readily see the connections between subjects such as math and science, or social studies and language arts. When selecting and analyzing evidence that will become artifacts for their portfolios, students recognize the relationships among these different content areas and are able to transfer learning from one context to another. The integration of curricular subjects becomes a natural by-product with e-portfolios' capacity to provide "hyperlinks" or "bookmarks" that move the viewer between and among the sections of the portfolio, providing easy access to audio and video clips.

This seamlessness in the e-portfolio (which can be achieved to a lesser degree in the paper portfolio) is what allows teachers to introduce the portfolio as a process that becomes the "metaphor" of each student's learning and achievement. When the capacity to self-reflect is applied to the e-portfolio the student is given the opportunity to project the picture of his or her academic "e-self." This has been recognized by the European Institute for E-Learning (2006), which that describes how the e-portfolio becomes a digital expression of the student's work and achievement.

STUDENT SELF-ASSESSMENT AND VOICE

The success of portfolio and e-portfolio processes depends greatly on the engagement of students in self-assessment. No matter what the purpose or type of the portfolio, teachers need to know how to assist students in learning how to identify, value, and assess their progress as individual learners. The increased use of portfolio procedures, as well as the writing process itself, has brought attention to the central importance of student voice in learning. When students are engaged in reflection on their work, and when they have the opportunity to "tell their stories" and participate in inquiry and self-assessment processes, they gain "agency." This has been defined as the capacity for human beings to make choices and then apply them. *Human agency* is an important self-attribute that effective educators inherently understand and try to foster in their students as steps toward success and lifelong learning (Holland, Lachicotte, Skinner, & Cain, 2001). Within the portfolio itself, voice enables the audience (or reader) to sense that the student, although not present, is speaking directly to the audience. The development of a strong sense of voice can be best ensured through the continuous processes of self-assessment and metacognition.

Self-assessment requires the skill referred to as *metacognition*, which is defined as a mental ability to think backwards or to reflect inwards. It corresponds to "intrapersonal intelligence," which cognitive psychologist Gardner (1993) values as the human capability to have an accurate understanding of one's self. (Students often understand this ability; when they do, they are described as being "self-smart.")

The portfolio process assists students in developing this intrapersonal intelligence through self-monitoring and inquiry. As students monitor and celebrate their growth and development in various curricular areas, they increase their metacognitive ability as well. They become responsible for directing their own learning—either individually or within cooperative work groups (Johnson & Johnson, 1996). Through peer engagement, coaching, and reflection, they recognize the interdependence of successful living and working in an ever-changing world. When teachers encourage students to critically evaluate their own work, those students become more independent and more self-confident learners. Students who engage in peer editing and review, portfolio conferences, and showcases develop the social and cognitive habits of mind that lead to success in academic study as well as in life. Just as the process of self-assessment that promotes student voice runs through the portfolio process, examples of self-reflection and assessment are found throughout the remaining chapters.

UNIVERSAL STANDARDS AND PORTFOLIOS

Academic standards help educators agree on a common vocabulary and common goals that transcend textbooks and curriculum guides. Regardless of where students live, what resources are available, or which teacher they have, students and parents know the knowledge, skills, and processes delineated by content area standards around the country that are important for each student to be successful. The universality of most standards cuts across geographical locations. Portfolios, whether print or digital, enable educators everywhere to bring the standards alive to students through meaningful work that is assessed authentically. Portfolios of standards-based work address the inconsistencies that belie the realities of trying to make one size fit all. As Carr and Harris (2001) state, "some standards are being taught but not assessed, assessed but not taught, or inconsistently taught and assessed within or across grade levels" (p. 5). Figure 3.4 demonstrates how standards for various disciplines can be taught and assessed within a standards-based portfolio process. (See Example 3.1 and Blacklines 3.1, 3.2, and 3.6 at the end of this chapter.)

STANDARDS-BASED PORTFOLIO PROMOTES STUDENT MOTIVATION

For a standards-based portfolio to be meaningful as well as effective, assessment tools such as checklists or scoring rubrics need to be carefully constructed so they can guide students' work. Ultimately, these same tools are included in the final portfolio as assessments that indicate whether the students have met or

Standards and Assessments

SOCIAL SCIENCE

Standard: Understand the development of significant political events.

Assessments:

1. Create a cause-and-effect graphic organizer for the American Revolution.
2. Compare and contrast the facts of an historical event and a fictional story about the event.

FINE ARTS—DANCE

Standard: Apply skills and knowledge necessary to create and perform in the arts.

Assessments:

1. Create a dance that demonstrates coordination, balance, and rhythmic response.
2. Demonstrate step patterns from different dance styles and forms.

FOREIGN LANGUAGE

Standard: Understand oral communication in the target language.

Assessments:

1. Rewrite a folktale from the target language to English.
2. Write and illustrate a recipe in the target language.

TECHNOLOGY

Standard: Use technology to locate, select, and manage information.

Assessments:

1. Create a reference list of Internet sources on an assigned topic.
2. Research a topic using three types of media.

Figure 3.4

exceeded the standard. When a student does not meet the standard during the portfolio process, the teacher helps the student to analyze the specific indicators of the assignment and to compare these to the student's work. This helps the student to recognize how the benchmark was missed and what the student needs to do in order to achieve it.

When students become active participants in the portfolio assessment process, they learn to use scoring rubrics as they complete assignments, and then assess themselves using the same rubric. This "self-inspection" process places students at the center of the assessment process, while providing them with knowledge, responsibility, and capability for improving and achieving the targeted standards.

Just as the "best work" portfolio that allows students to select their very best work improves their self-esteem and impresses their parents at back-to-school night, the standards-based portfolio promotes student motivation and willingness to apply more rigor in their work and to become responsible for higher achievement. (See Example 3.2 and Blackline 3.3 at the end of this chapter.)

ORGANIZING ENTRIES FOR
THE STANDARDS PORTFOLIO

Teachers need a carefully thought-out plan to help students organize their work for a standards portfolio. For example, if using a paper portfolio process, students can organize the loose assignments more efficiently if each is given a three-inch-wide hanging folder. They then write their names on the outside of the hanging folder into which they insert separate folders, each a different color and labeled with the standard to be addressed. These folders are labeled so that students and teachers can file each assignment according to the standard it addresses. When an assignment meets several subject area standards a separate folder may be used, or it can be filed by the principal standard that is met. Teachers can use file cabinets or plastic milk crates to efficiently store students' hanging folders.

When items are sent home for parent or guardian review, students can be instructed to return them with their comments, to be included in the working folders (see Figure 3.5). When children are in the primary grades, a reflection form for parents and guardians can accompany this work. This will promote two-way communication and inform caregivers about the standards that are being addressed and the progress the student is making toward achievement.

Rough drafts along with final copies, graded papers, rewrites, and pictures of projects and performances are among the items that can be selected for the

---

Sample Note to Parents

Dear Parents,

On your child's desk for Open House, you will notice a project called a "Showcase Portfolio." This portfolio contains your child's selections from this year's accumulated work, which includes writing, reading logs, photos of work in progress, social studies and science journals, as well as a potpourri of other items of importance to him or her. Each item in the portfolio contains a personal "reflection" on why the work is important, what change has occurred as a result of this work, and what degree of growth the work represents.

Portfolios are a relatively new idea in education designed to go beyond just collecting work, to reflecting on the work that has been collected. You will notice sets of questions in the portfolio, designed to address different types of work. In the future, portfolios may be one of the means used by the state for assessment purposes.

This year, the children and I have used portfolios to assess personal change—this year's classroom "theme." As a result, all of the work in your child's portfolio is a "showcase" of what your child considers important in demonstrating growth as a learner. There were few limitations and controls put on the contents of the body of work. All children made their own choices.

Please take the time to go through the portfolio with your child. I would appreciate it if you would take the time to respond to the attached "Parent Reflections" page, in much the same way as your child did on the "Student Reflections" pages.

If you wish, consider writing a letter to your child, as your child did to you when presenting the portfolio. Your letters, or reflections, may be put in the portfolio tray on my desk, to be delivered to your child tomorrow.

Thank you for your time and support.

Sincerely,

Mrs. Adelman

Figure 3.5

standards-based portfolio or e-portfolio. The student completes a portfolio or e-portfolio artifact reflection and includes it with the final piece, the scoring rubric or checklist completed by the teacher (and student), and the student's reflection about the artifact. Together, these pieces create a portfolio that offers concrete evidence that the standard was addressed; provides the student-produced document that proves that the student achieved the objective of the assignment; includes the checklist or scoring rubric that describes the level at which the student met the standard; and includes the student's stated rationale as to the value of the work or the learning process used to attain it. Figure 3.6 provides an example of an artifact that includes these four components.

Earth Science Student Checklist

Third-Grade Standards

Students will investigate the physical attributes of rocks and soil.

Criteria/Performance Indicators: The student can	Not Yet 0	Some Evidence 1
Explain the differences between a rock and mineral		
• How are rocks and minerals similar?		
• How are rocks and minerals different?		
Recognize the physical attributes of rocks using		
• Observation (shape, color, texture)		
• Measurement		
• Simple tests (hardness)		
Recognize the physical attributes of minerals using		
• Observation (shape, color, texture)		
• Measurement		
• Simple tests (hardness)		
Use observation to compare the similarities and differences of topsoils such as clay, loam, potting soil, and sand according to		
• Texture		
• Particle		
• Size		
• Color		
Determine how water and wind can change rocks and soil over time using		
• Observation		
• Research		

Figure 3.6

One method of documenting students' meeting each standard is to write the specific standard at the top of each entry. Figure 3.7 shows a primary example of student reflection on an artifact that meets a math standard.

Middle school language arts teachers—responsible for helping students meet four standards related to reading, writing, speaking, and listening—can require students to list the appropriate standard at the top of each piece of work and file them in separate folders. This type of accountability system helps teachers, parents, and students monitor progress to make sure all of the standards are taught and assessed.

STANDARDS AND CRITERIA CHECKLISTS

Most state standards provide educators with specific descriptors, indicators, or criteria that delineate what needs to be included in a sample of student work. Some states or provinces, however, provide only the standards, without providing details. As students acquire familiarity with learning standards and become skillful in applying their own benchmarks of learning to these standards, the portfolio or e-portfolio enables them to link their artifacts to the standards posted on local, state, or province Web sites. In any case, teachers must be able to design their own criteria to help students complete the standards-based assignments in ways that are both helpful and meaningful to students.

Teachers will often find support for identifying the criteria for student projects and performances in their curriculum guides, but these guides are

Primary Integrated Language Arts Student Reflection

Self-Portrait

I like my picture because I made it all by myself

Food Turkey

I like my food turkey because it is made out of food and it makes me want to eat it all up.

Figure 3.7

SOURCE: S. Silverman Web page (http://kids-learn.org/).

Sample Standards and Assessments

Language Arts

The student produces a narrative account.

Assessments

1. A news account of an event in history

2. A biographical account of a famous American

3. A travel diary of a trip

Mathematics

The student demonstrates and applies geometric concepts involving points, lines, planes, and space.

Assessments

1. Drawings of two-dimensional shapes

2. Drawings of circle and sphere, square and cube, triangle and pyramid

3. Pictures of art, advertising, and construction that show geometric figures

Health

The student can explain the basic principles of health promotion, illness prevention, and safety.

Assessments

1. Pamphlet related to a specific disease (symptoms, preventions, treatments)

2. Report on safety methods that reduce risks (wearing seat belts, wearing helmets, using sunscreen)

Science

The student knows and applies the concepts, principles, and processes of scientific inquiry.

Assessments

1. Formulate questions on a science topic and select five steps to answer questions.

2. Collect data and construct a chart to display data.

3. Give an oral report on reasonable explanations.

Figure 3.8

sometimes too broad or generic. When teachers set out to create their own descriptive checklists that guide students to meet the standard, they begin with the standard's outcome (as described) and work backwards. This process is found in the example of a middle school language arts standard. By using the performance descriptors from the standard, teachers can pull the criteria that should help students produce "a narrative account" (Figure 3.8).

Since the resultant descriptors or criteria might be too overwhelming to promote in one assignment, teachers have found that by clustering or "chunking" the criteria into sequential order (Figure 3.9) students can progress in a logical order and complete one step at a time.

Checklist for a Narrative Standard		
Performance Descriptors	Not Yet 0	Some Evidence 1
Engages Reader		
Context of story		
Reader interest		
Establishes a Situation		
Plot		
Point of view		
Setting		
Conflict		
Creates an Organizing Structure		
Topic sentence		
Support sentence		
Transitions		
Motif/theme		
Symbolism		
Develops Complex Characters		
Protagonist		
Antagonist		
Dialogue		
Creates Sensory Details		
Descriptive language		
Figurative language		

Figure 3.9

CHECKLISTS AS GUIDEPOSTS

As shown, standards that include specific indicators and criteria facilitate the creation of checklists because they provide teachers with key words or concepts to include in the checklists. Teachers can also create their own student-friendly checklists that guide their students in the completion of a task. For example, teachers in a California elementary school developed a checklist to help their fourth-grade students produce a report on the rivers of California (Figure 3.10).

Report on California Rivers Checklist

CA Social Studies Standard 4.1: Students demonstrate an understanding of the physical and human geographic features that define places and regions in California. Identify the locations of the Pacific Ocean, rivers, valleys, and mountain passes, and explain their effects on the growth of towns.

CA Language Arts Standard 2.1: Make narrative presentations: (a) Relate ideas, observations, or recollections about an event or experience. (b) Provide a context that enables the listener to imagine the circumstances of the event or experience. (c) Provide insight into why the selected event or experience is memorable.

Assignment: Complete a research report on the rivers of California.

Step 1. Research:

Gather information from three different sources.

- Internet
- Historical fiction
- Social studies textbook
- Charts, maps, etc.
- Resource books
- Other: _____

Step 2. Understand facts about geographic location.

- Location in state
- Historical importance
- Agriculture
- Characteristics
- Other: _____

Step 3. Organize information from three different sources.

- Notes
- Models or maps
- Outline
- Graphic organizers

Step 4. Present information orally.

- Note cards
- Electronic presentation
- Displays—charts, maps, etc.

Figure 3.10

This checklist demonstrates how teachers can guide students through each step in the process to write a research report. Since writing a subject area report requires research, the students first have to check off and sometimes write in the information they have gathered. If students complete the entire checklist, they will do a better job on their written report. Teachers often ask the students to staple the checklist to their final draft before placing it in their working folder. The checklist provides an efficient way for both students and teachers to monitor progress toward completing the task.

RUBRICS

The major problem with attaching only a checklist to an artifact that may become a portfolio entry is that it may not fully indicate the quality of the work and how it met or exceeded the standards. Students may have indicated that they included an item on the checklist, but the item may not exhibit the quality of the artifact. A student may include an introductory sentence to a script for an oral report, but what if it is poorly written and has no relationship to the topic? A scoring rubric spells out what makes an effective introduction to a main idea and, most important, whether or not that work meets or exceeds the standard. On a rubric that is either co-constructed by students or presented to them at the outset of an assigned performance, students can see exactly what they have to do to move forward on the continuum toward quality work.

The narrative account rubric (Figure 3.11) utilizes the clustered checklist in Figure 3.10 to determine criteria, but expands the criteria by generating descriptors and ratings for each criterion so students know how they rate and what they need to do to improve their narrative piece.

PORTFOLIO VERSUS COLLECTION OF "STUFF"

In today's age of accountability, collecting student work, placing it in a folder, and showing it to administrators and parents is not sufficient proof that the teacher has covered the curriculum and the student has mastered the standards. As we have previously mentioned, a standards-based portfolio contains student work correlated to curriculum goals, aligned to standards, and assessed with checklists and scoring rubrics. It not only provides concrete evidence of students' progress toward meeting or exceeding goals, but it also includes student "voice" that is written with print portfolios or captured through recorded audio or video clips with e-portfolios. The standards-based portfolio, therefore, ensures a more systematic and structured approach to assessment *of* and *for* learning, and provides a rich opportunity for students and their teachers to monitor their achievement and set goals for their learning continuum.

As Popham (1999) states, "Teachers who adopt portfolios in their classrooms will make the ongoing collection and appraisal of students' work a central focus of the instructional program rather than a peripheral activity whereby students occasionally gather up their work to convince a teacher's supervisor or students' parents that good things have been going on in class" (p. 182). (See Blackline 3.4 at the end of this chapter.) Portfolios—especially standards-based portfolios—provide more than a scrapbook to share on back-to-school night. They document students' learning, and support the grading system that evaluates students'

Rubric for California Rivers Presentation

Criteria	Below Standards 1	Almost Meets Standards 2	Meets Standards 3	Exceeds Standards 4
Information	• No evidence of sources.	• Fewer than three sources	• Three different sources.	• Three different sources.
Geographic Location Facts	• Few relevant geographic facts are presented.	• Some relevant geographic facts are presented.	• Most facts presented reflect the location in the state, historical importance, agriculture, and other characteristics.	• Facts are presented about the location in the state, historical importance, agriculture, and other characteristics.
Organization Tools	• Use of organization tools is minimal or not apparent.	• Information is organized from fewer that three different sources including notes, outlines, graphic organizers, models or maps.	• Information is organized from at least three different sources including notes, outlines, graphic organizers, models or maps.	• Information is organized from three or more different sources including notes, outlines, graphic organizers models or maps.
Present Information Orally • Language and vocabulary • Visual aids • Technology	• Language and vocabulary are not appropriate to purpose. • No visual aids. • No technology.	• Language and vocabulary are somewhat appropriate to purpose. • Few visual aids. • Technology is used.	• Language and vocabulary are appropriate to purpose. • Some visual aids. • Technology is used to enhanced the oral presentation.	• Excellent use of language and vocabulary that are appropriate to purpose. • Many well-designed visual aids. • Exceptional use of technology.

Student Comment:	Scale
	15–16 = A 12–14 = B
Teacher Comment:	8–11 = C Below 8 = Not yet

Figure 3.11

progress or lack of progress in achieving academic goals. Portfolios also help teachers monitor their own effectiveness in teaching skills necessary for students to achieve deep understanding of essential knowledge.

Middle School Student Reflection on Rivers of California Presentation

In this assignment I worked with my team to collect information about the rivers of California. I learned that rivers are important to our lives.

We need rivers for water to drink and to water the crops that are grown in California. Because we have not taken care of the rivers, some have dried up for most of the year, or they are just really small. Sometimes we dump waste into our rivers that makes them sick and we can't use them to drink or even swim.

Most of California's rivers are beautiful and people just like to camp or hike near them.

We learned that we have to take care of California rivers so that kids that live here after us can enjoy them too.

Figure 3.12

Examples

• • •

Rubric for Narrative Writing

Criteria	Below Standards 1	Almost Meets Standards 2	Meets Standards 3	Exceeds Standards 4
Engages Reader				
• Context	No context	Context is confusing	Context sets the scene for the story	Context develops a framework for the story
• Reader Interest	Does not engage reader	Attempts to engage reader	Captures the reader's attention	Grips the reader throughout narrative
Establishes a Situation				
• Plot	No evidence of plot	Plot is confusing and/or doesn't make sense	Plot is developed coherently	Plot provides surprising twists
• Point of View	Vague point of view	Varies from 1st, 2nd, to 3rd person	Shifts from 1st person to 3rd person on occasion	Uses appropriate point of view consistently and effectively
• Setting	Not provided	Provides place <u>or</u> time	Provides place <u>and</u> time	Vividly describes both place and time
• Conflict	No conflict	Rising action	• Rising action • Climax	• Rising action • Climax • Denouement
Creates an Organizing Structure				
• Topic Sentence	None	Wrong main idea	Correct and controlling main idea	Clear and powerful main idea
• Support Sentence	Sentences do not relate to topic sentence	1 supporting sentence related to topic	2 supporting sentences related to topic	3 or more well-written supporting sentences
• Transitions	No transitions	Basic transitions (and, but . . .) used appropriately	Varied transitions (however, moreover, therefore . . .) used	Skillful use of transitional words and phrases to connect ideas
• Motif/ Theme	No evidence	Vague theme—not fully developed	Theme woven throughout	Theme appropriately conveys author's message
• Symbolism	No symbols	Vague use of one symbol—not fully developed	1 to 2 appropriate symbols woven throughout	1 to 2 effective symbols that contribute significantly to the meaning of the story

Criteria	Below Standards 1	Almost Meets Standards 2	Meets Standards 3	Exceeds Standards 4
Develops Complex Characters				
• Protagonist	Not fully developed	Stereotypical "good guy"(no surprises)	Fully developed main character	Complex and empathetic main character
• Antagonist	Not fully developed	Stereotypical "bad guy" (no surprises)	Fully developed foil to main character	Complex foil to main character
• Dialogue	Little or not dialogue among characters	Stilted dialogue that does not fully develop characters	Realistic dialogue appropriate to characters—advances plot line	Colorful dialogue with use of appropriate dialect, idioms, slang
Creates Sensory Details				
• Descriptive Language	Lacks specific descriptions	Word choice is bland and nondescript	Use of descriptive adjectives	Vivid use of descriptive words that "paint a picture" in the mind
• Figurative Language	No figurative language	Use of simile *or* metaphor	Use of simile *and* metaphor	Creative use of similes and metaphors
	Nondescript language	Use of appropriate vocabulary	Action verbs and colorful adjectives	Vivid word usage enhances narrative
Clasure				
• Foreshadowing	No evidence	1 obvious hint	2 hints	3 or more subtle hints
• Story Ending	No ending/or inappropriate ending—no foreshadowing	Unsatisfying ending—loose ends (weak foreshadowing)	Ending provides closure to story—evidence of foreshadowing	Cleverly foreshadowed surprise ending

Comments: _____

_____

_____

Signed: _____ Date: _____

Points	Scale
19–25	Below Standards
26–45	Almost Meets Standards
46–65	Meets Standards
66–76	Exceeds Standards

Example 3.1

The How

Select items for the portfolio that meet state goals in science.

Student: ___Matt___   Grade/Class: __8__   Date: __3/15__

Standards	Portfolio Entry	Date Completed
Know basic vocabulary of biological science	Vocabulary test	10/3
Know implications and limitations of technical development	Book report on *Brave New World*	11/15
Know principles of scientific research	Journal entry	1/22
Know processes of science	Lab report on experiment	2/9

Example 3.2

Blacklines

●●●

Clustered Criteria Checklist

Standard: _____

Assignment: _____

Criteria/Performance Indicators	Not Yet 0	Some Evidence 1
•		
•		
•		
•		
•		
•		
•		
•		
•		
•		
•		
•		
•		
•		
•		

Blackline 3.1

Clustered Checklist–Standard

Name: _____ Date: _____

Standard: _____

Performance Indicators: _____

Cluster the indicators into five areas.

Criteria/Performance Indicators	Not Yet 0	Some Evidence 1
[ ]		
•		
•		
•		
[ ]		
•		
•		
•		
[ ]		
•		
•		
•		
[ ]		
•		
•		
•		
[ ]		
•		
•		
Comments:		

Blackline 3.2

Standards Log

List the standards, then list the portfolio entries that address each standard.

Student: _____ **Grade/Class:** _____ **Date:** _____

Standards	Portfolio Entry	Date Completed

Blackline 3.3

Portfolio Selection

Date: _____

To: Parent/Significant Other

In preparation for the standards portfolio your student _____ will be
(student's name)
presenting at the end of this semester, we would like to seek your feedback. Please review the attached entries with corresponding standards and talk with your student about the work that has been completed. Also respond to the questions below that assist your student in reflecting on his or her achievement.

Please review the attached entries that may be included in _____'s
portfolio and provide your feedback. (student's name)

Which piece most surprises you? Why?

Which piece do you feel needs more work? Why?

Which piece do you want to include in the portfolio? Why?

Signature: _____

Date: _____

Blackline 3.4

Portfolio Schedule for the Year

Dates	Event

Blackline 3.5

Artifact Selection on Integrated Subject Evidence

Student Name: _____   Date: _____

The What

Primary Subject Area: _____

Standard: State what standard has been met? _____

Second Subject Area: _____

Standard: State what standard has been met? _____

Third Subject Area: _____

Standard: State what standard has been met? _____

_____

The How

What evidence does this show?

Primary Subject Assessment: _____

Second Subject Assessment: _____

Third Subject Assessment: _____

_____

The Why

Your statement of why the pieces show that you met each of the standards:

_____

_____

_____

Blackline 3.6

4

Connect Portfolio Purpose Through Students' Collections, Reflections, and Selections

The heart of a successful portfolio or e-portfolio is the ongoing involvement of students in performance-based instruction, as well as in more formal assessment experiences. Portfolios, in coordination with quizzes and tests, offer an ideal context for monitoring students' own reflections on the completion of assigned tasks and complex performances. When students are well prepared for this stage, they are able to record their ongoing reflections and keep track of goal-setting or decision-making processes. Connecting to other students through ongoing peer review and evaluation helps them to gain multicultural perspective and respect for the diversity of others. The key to achieving this is through employing the two most important aspects of the portfolio preparation process: order and organization.

Teachers who would like to initiate student portfolios in their classrooms, departments, or grade levels must address two questions: (1) "How do you make sure that students are connected to the purpose of the portfolio?" and (2) "How can students acquire the ability to self-assess and value the specific evidence of work to be included?"

After defining the purpose of the portfolio or targeting the standards, curriculum goals, or portfolio objectives to be addressed, the system of portfolio development begins. This is when students are introduced to the portfolio and the ongoing process of gathering, collecting, and reflecting on artifacts of their work. The preparations that teachers make before this have included

1. making the necessary decisions about the purpose of the portfolio as well as the type of container it will use (digital, notebook, box, file folder, or photo album);

2. deciding on the organization (table of contents or artifact registry);

3. determining the labeling technique (tabs, links, dividers);

4. establishing the order of artifact presentation (standards or objectives, title and grade level, chronological or subject-matter sequence, reflective statement); and

5. designing the overall look of the collection. (See Chapter 3.)

6. Consideration of how the portfolio will be presented to the audience is introduced at this stage and will be covered in more depth in Chapter 6.

All of these decisions shape the organization of the portfolio and provide a sense of order that will guide students as they become the owners, designers, and artists of their portfolios. If in the early stages teachers keep the number and variety of portfolio or e-portfolio artifacts to a manageable number, order will likely reign over chaos in the later stages when the amount of material can easily increase. When this sense of order guides the entire portfolio process, students will quickly adopt a sense of self-efficacy and initiative in identifying, storing, and reviewing the items they wish to include in the portfolio.

INTRODUCTION

"A portfolio is a purposeful collection of student work that exhibits the student's efforts, progress, and achievements in one or more areas" (Paulson et al., 1991, p. 60). A digital portfolio (or e-portfolio) is this and more. Because of the platform of computer technology and communication, e-portfolios can more visibly support students in their learning process.

Most teachers realize that portfolios demonstrate what students know and what they can do. They also realize that they "can gain a better understanding of a student's abilities and accomplishments by simply looking at the student's work, rather than the abstracted final grade" (Niquida, 1993, p. 1). They also believe that portfolios complement paper-and-pencil tests as formative tools that measure academic skills and help the teachers make informed instructional decisions. By using portfolios and e-portfolios, students are able to take ownership as they begin to "compile their best work in writing, math, science, art (and even community service) to present a more vivid record of what they are able to do" (Niquida, p. 1). This chapter focuses on teachers' concern with logistics: "How is it possible to collect all the 'stuff' from all of my students, organize it into a portfolio system, and still maintain my sanity?" It also addresses ways in which parents are brought into the portfolio process from development of purpose through the promotion of individual student voice.

While it is true that portfolios will take more time and more planning, teachers recognize that the payoff in terms of student motivation, involvement in self-assessment, goal setting, and overall achievement is worth it. Meaningful portfolio projects do not just happen. Portfolios place additional demands on teachers and students (as well as on parents). In addition, e-portfolios can often stretch technological and instructional resources. Even though teachers, parents, administrators, and students may find the journey of developing and preparing for a meaningful portfolio process to be challenging and time consuming, it is ultimately rewarding and satisfying for all.

COLLECTIONS

Many educators believe that children in the early primary grades are not capable of participating in a meaningful portfolio process, but teachers in prekindergarten through third-grade classrooms who have implemented portfolios and authentic assessments with young children disprove this belief.

- Our youngest children take to the portfolio process amazingly easily. They love the attention of looking at their work and products of their artistic abilities. They inherently understand what their "best" work is; when asked about it, they will honestly tell if they worked hard on a piece, or if it is their favorite.
- Even kindergarten-age children can participate in the portfolio selection process. They enjoy working with teacher assistants or parent volunteers to look at pieces in their "working folder." They enjoy sharing informally within small groups in the classroom as well.
- First-grade children love the entire portfolio process. They understand how to select portfolio pieces. Their new independence in reading and writing increases their enjoyment of celebrating their growth.

Teachers of students in the intermediate and middle school grades also find the challenges of promoting organization and order in the portfolio process to be daunting yet doable. Following the development of purpose, and after students have begun to fully participate in the portfolio process, teachers note that "using student portfolios has definitely increased my students' motivation, but with 100-plus students I find the organizational aspect to be a nightmare!"

High school teachers have found that students have an affinity for collecting "stuff." (Just look at their bedroom closets or school lockers.) Many adults tend to believe that they have trouble organizing their things. Yet with guidance and involvement of students in the portfolio process, teachers have found that students can be very successful in maintaining the necessary order. As with earlier grades, if time has been taken to develop a coherent process that addresses the logistics of an undertaking of this magnitude, secondary teachers and their students are likely to enjoy success.

The following options for storage, organizational flow, and organizational tools need to be considered in developing a portfolio plan at any grade level.

STORAGE AND MATERIALS FOR THE PAPER PORTFOLIO

Cereal Boxes—Snap, Crackle, Pop

Preprimary and elementary teachers like to use large cereal boxes to hold their students' work. They write students' names on the side panel and store the boxes upright on a shelf as if they were books. The students decorate the front and back of the boxes with artwork or collages. The box then serves as an inexpensive working folder before items are selected to meet the purpose and goals of the final portfolio.

An easy and inexpensive way to create the final portfolio container for students at this level is to use two large pieces of 18" × 24" heavyweight tagboard. Evenly fold the second piece around the bottom of the first piece. Seal on three sides, leaving the top open for storage. Fold the entire board in half. This results in a double-sided pocket folder that is easily handled and that accommodates four subject areas for each young student.

Hanging Files—Hang It Up

Teachers set up hanging files for each student to serve as a working portfolio that contains all the student's work. Students keep all of their work in the hanging files stored in a file cabinet, milk crate, or box. Plastic milk crates make excellent portable portfolio systems if file cabinets are not available or if teachers have to switch classrooms.

Notebooks—Book It

Students in the intermediate and upper grades can keep a three-hole notebook binder with separate dividers or pocket folders for pieces of work. The pocket folders store artifacts, cassettes, or videos. Plastic protectors can also be used to hold rough drafts as well as final copies. Rough drafts and final copies show growth and provide ways to measure improvement over time.

RAINBOW COLLECTION—RAINBOWING

Students can separate their work into colored folders according to subject areas, works in progress, best work, "not yet" work, group work, or integrated assignments (Figure 4.1). These folders are stored in file cabinets, student desks, or student notebooks. Colored folders can help organize a standards-based portfolio system by designating different subject areas. Or the colored folders could designate standards that have been exceeded, standards that have been met, and standards that still need to be met.

Red = Language arts
Blue = Math
Yellow = Science
Green = Social studies

Figure 4.1

Folders—Accordion Pleats

Large folders with accordion pleats can contain large samples, artifacts, or projects. These can also hold cassette tapes, art, videos, CDs, file folders, notebooks, and larger group projects that require more space than a file folder or binder can provide.

Media Center—Bank Vault

Class or schoolwide portfolios, integrated portfolios, or multiyear portfolios can be placed in accordion-pleated folders and stored in the media center for easy access and review. Students may check out their portfolios as needed, especially for updates of the registry, revisions, and conferences to monitor their growth and development over time.

Photo Albums—Portphotos

Photo albums, or portphotos, can be used at all levels to showcase pictures of student projects, group skits, performances, field trips, travels, extracurricular activities, commendations, awards, hobbies, programs from school concerts or plays, articles from school or local newspapers, invitations to events, and ticket stubs from sporting or cultural events. These artifacts provide insight into a student's life, both inside and outside of school. The portphotos can portray the "whole" student through the integration of academic, extracurricular, and social activities. The portphotos can be used by students to creatively display evidence of their engagement in any number of projects or performances.

The Creative Portfolio

When the purpose of the portfolio is to demonstrate student achievement of several concepts, skills, procedures, or knowledge from many subject areas, some teachers have led children in the development of creative portfolios. Adelman (1992) shows that portfolios that re-create the theme of the unit or integrated theme project can be highly motivating and successful for students.

The E-portfolio Tools and Storage

When teachers plan to utilize technology to design and implement e-portfolios they need to consider how to provide access by all learners and stakeholders—teachers, parents, prospective evaluators, and so on—while planning to protect some or all aspects of students' identity and work. This can be accomplished by storing student digital files on an Intranet with an electronic key or password, or students might be given space on the secure district server. Alternatively, students can be provided with storage devices such as USB drives, audiotapes, or DVDs or CDs. Many teachers prefer the e-portfolio since it easily captures, stores, displays [as well as] retrieves and deletes information and materials that are to be included (Bergmann, 2004). With ever-developing technological storage devices, teachers must decide wisely on the most secure, dependable, and accessible media for storage of student work and portfolio contents.

The e-portfolio has recently become the container of choice because it has the capability to accommodate multiple forms of electronic multimedia. Bergmann (2004) describes a wide range of formats that the e-portfolio maintains: "static text and graphic displays, databases, audio bites, video clips, panoramic files, object oriented (three-dimensional) files, virtual reality, etc." (p. 6).

Teachers using digital media as the containers for storage of students' artifacts will require their students to download to a storage device or save and upload written work; problem-solving logs; journals and presentations; and projects and the scoring rubrics that accompany them to an Intranet or secure school district server. The e-portfolio then becomes a flexible system for capturing and showcasing evidence of student achievement. We cannot overemphasize that the accessibility of the contents of an e-portfolio that contains items from students' cumulative folder must be monitored carefully and continuously for security and confidentiality. (See Examples 4.2 and 4.6 at the end of this chapter.)

Organizational Flow of the Portfolio and E-portfolio

If order guides portfolio development in the early stages when the number and variety of artifacts are manageable, then order will reign over eliminate the possibility of chaos in the later stages when the amount of material can easily become unmanageable. Although a comprehensive portfolio incorporates many steps, the three essential steps in this chapter—collect, select, reflect—remain crucial to the portfolio's organizational flow (see Figure 4.2). Students will need direction and support to collect relevant items, select key items that meet goals or purposes, and reflect on the importance of the items in relationship to their goals. When teachers develop a logical organizational system that helps students take early control of their portfolios, the entire process will be more manageable, more meaningful, and more satisfying for all their students. (See Blackline 4.1 at the end of this chapter.)

The following tools help all students organize and chronicle their work:

Working Folder–Collectibles

Often teachers have students collect everything they do in class and save it in a "working folder." Sometimes teachers do not know the portfolio requirements in advance, so they ask students to save everything until it is time to organize the artifacts by standard, curriculum goal, topic, or subject area. The working

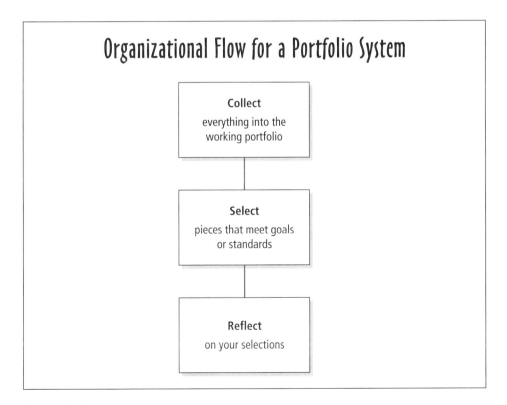

Figure 4.2

paper portfolio could be a hanging file, notebook, cereal box, or any large container that can store papers, projects, cassettes, and videotapes. The working e-portfolio is essentially electronic folders saved in devices (writeable CDs or flash drives), or, if provided by the school, Web space on the district server.

After students collect specific work and store it in the appropriate container, the process is only one-third completed. The collection process can take a week, several weeks, a quarter, a semester, or a year, depending on the purpose of the portfolio and the appropriate time frame determined by teachers. Many items will involve student choice, whereas some items could involve teacher selection focused on school accountability demands. After the collection stage, students will be guided to the *selection* stage. Figure 4.3 lists what students might collect.

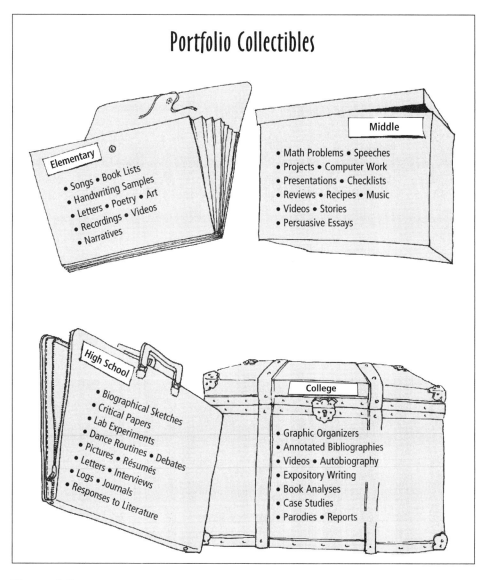

Figure 4.3

Final Portfolio—Reflectibles

Even though teachers may require certain entries to be included in the academic portfolios, students also select entries called "free picks" to be included. In the selection process, students reflect on and describe their selections while using criteria from learning standards, scoring rubrics, or checklists to show what they have learned and achieved. (See Example 4.3 at the end of this chapter for a sample organizational flow.)

ORGANIZATIONAL TOOLS

Like the construction and design of a work of art, the portfolio's physical setup helps familiarize the student and the audience with its purpose. It also promotes understanding of the reasons for selection and presentation of the pieces. Teachers and students need to develop familiarity with a number of organizational tools in order to identify and utilize those that will make the portfolio user-friendly for the student and other interested parties.

Dividers—Tabs and Dabs

Divided notebook folders or plastic divider pages are useful in separating work by genre or subject area, rough drafts and final drafts, best work and "not yet" pieces, individual work or group work. Dividers also separate the portfolio according to the table of contents. Tabs allow students and their audiences to quickly move around the paper portfolio to access specific pieces. Similarly, the e-portfolio can be formatted with "bookmarks" and "hyperlinks" that promote easy readability and navigation among the different parts of the portfolio.

Colored Dots—Dotted Swiss

Colored dots in all sizes can be used to code entries in the portfolio (Figure 4.4). The coding helps students recognize what still needs to be completed or improved. The dots help the student with organization during the design process; they are often removed at the time for presentation. Sometimes the dots are kept to assist the audience in understanding the organization of the portfolio. In this instance, a code for the dots needs to be included in the portfolio's table of contents.

Colored Dot Codes

Yellow dot = First draft

Green dot = Second draft

Red dot = Final draft

Blue dot = Reflection

Black dot = Meets standard

Figure 4.4

Table of Contents—Table It

A table of contents is necessary in portfolios and e-portfolios because it lists all of the entries and corresponding sections, page numbers, or electronic bookmarks. Most final portfolios contain between seven and ten well-selected items. Approximately seven items represent student work related to the purposes (goals or standards). Entries such as a reflection page, a student self-assessment, and a goal-setting page complete the final portfolio by incorporating thoughtful insight into the student's academic strengths and learning challenges.

Artifact Registry—Hotel Registry

Portfolio registries chronicle when and why students remove items (eject) and replace them with newer items (inject) (Dietz, 1992). Useful in paper portfolios and e-portfolios, the artifact registry includes the dates, items, and reasons for removal and replacement of artifacts. The ongoing process of a registry reinforces students' metacognition, because they are encouraged to engage in "thinking about their own thinking" and learning as they complete the registry. Students using the artifact registry for e-portfolios can efficiently enter anecdotal records and dates on the entries that they reflect upon and select for continued inclusion in the portfolio. (See Example 4.4 and Blackline 4.3 at the end of this chapter.)

Self-Assessment Stems—Self-Checks

As has been stated several times in previous chapters, the promotion of student voice through reflection, self-assessment, and goal setting in the portfolio process is critical. Students empowered to self-assess their knowledge, their progress, and their mastery of the purposes, goals, or standards within the portfolio process develop into independent and self-sufficient learners. As the process unfolds, students who are better able to assess their own work based on predetermined criteria and indicators will likely become more critical thinkers. When teachers promote student capability in both using and designing scoring rubrics that are based on the key criteria required for successful achievement, students become more likely to meet or exceed benchmarks. Because portfolio artifacts are accompanied by dated scoring rubrics that have been used throughout the year, all stakeholders who review students' progress will be able to see the story behind the way in which they have achieved academic goals.

Biography of a Work Log—Bed to Bed

Wolf (1989) says that long-term projects require "moment-to-moment monitoring, Monday morning quarterbacking, and countless judgments of errors and worth" (p. 35). A biography of a work traces the development of a major project or performance. This is why it is frequently used by teachers in elementary and secondary classrooms as a kind of miniportfolio. The biography lists dated entries and chronicles the development of an idea from its inception to the final product or performance—metaphorically, from getting up in the morning to going to bed in the evening. The biography of a work log attached to the final product helps the student (and the portfolio audience) recognize the entry point or diagnostic benchmark and the progress he or she has made toward achieving an academic goal. Similarly, a biography of a work log provides the audience with a bigger picture of how the student developed as a reader, writer, thinker, and so on in the process of completing the particular piece of work. (See Blacklines 4.2 and 4.4 at the end of this chapter.)

Index—Let Your Fingers Do the Walking

It is sometimes helpful if students compile an alphabetical index of major items that can be added at the end of their portfolios. An index serves as an easy reference for specific examples that show evidence of writing skills, multiple intelligences, group work, artwork, extracurricular activities, content, or standards.

Sticky Notes—Note Post

Students want and need feedback on their work. Formal feedback for portfolios includes an evaluation form or scoring rubric, while informal feedback includes comments that can be written on sticky notes. Using removable notes means that the students' original work is not violated and grades or comments are privately read by the student. The students can review notes and then remove them before sharing the portfolio formally with parents, peers, or visitors during an exhibition portfolio exhibition or showcase.

The e-portfolio version of the sticky note is the comment insertion function that is available in most of the major word processing software programs. Comments placed throughout artifacts of students' portfolios can be printed out, along with the artifact content for the student's review and then deleted for upcoming online showcases or exhibitions.

Artifact Entry Sheets—Entry Captions

It is possible that a student can become overwhelmed with the amount of materials, media, and papers to be included when transferring work from a working folder to a final portfolio. If this occurs, it can be difficult and time consuming to organize the final portfolio. It is wise to assist students in the early stages of artifact collection to complete and attach an *artifact entry sheet* to any item that they believe should ultimately be included in the portfolio. By placing the necessary information on the artifact "cover sheet," the students will have everything they will later need to identify the item for inclusion in the portfolio or e-portfolio. (See Figure 4.5 for a sample cover sheet, and Example 4.4 at the end of this chapter.)

Sample Portfolio Entry Sheet

Name of Student: _Michael_

Date of Entry: _5/18_

Title or Description of Entry: _Narrative Paper on Most Embarrassing Moment_

Standard Addressed: _Writing Standard E-2_

Why This Entry Is Important: _I think it is humorous and I worked hard on keeping my verb tense consistent and keeping the reader's interest._

Personal Reflection: _I spent a lot of time on this paper because I knew I had to read it to the class. I enjoyed writing this because it made my friends laugh._

Figure 4.5

THE PORTFOLIO SELECTION PROCESS

Several important questions about portfolios arise during the selection process:

> What should be included?
>
> How will the items be selected?
>
> Who will select the items?
>
> When will these items be selected?

During the collection phase, many students can become pack rats and accumulate large masses of papers, media, and projects in a working folder. Because of this possibility, it is important for teachers to keep students focused on the organizational structure and tools of the selection process. Without an understanding of the entire portfolio process, many teachers have concluded that the collection *only* is the final portfolio. They forget or do not realize that the second important step in an academic portfolio is *selection*—the stage at which students prune away the items that don't meet the criteria in favor of those that *meet or exceed* the purpose for which the portfolio has been designed.

The selection process will link the portfolio more specifically to the purpose that has been earlier decided. The purpose of the portfolio determines what items to select for the final or showcase portfolio. If the purpose of the portfolio is to meet standards, then artifacts need to be selected because they show clear and compelling evidence that they meet the standards. If the purpose of the portfolio is to show best work, then representative pieces for each type of work need to be included. In a writing portfolio, for example, narratives, expository pieces, persuasive letters, and journal entries, as well as literary critiques should link directly to each goal or standard.

Selection and Assessment

As detailed earlier, teachers designing effective portfolio processes establish and formalize the use of scoring criteria at the beginning. They have decided if general guidelines or more specific criteria for assignments or signature pieces are appropriate. Decisions about who selects the artifacts, and how and when the selections are made must be determined in advance. The focus of the selection process is on determining what entries need to be culled from a working portfolio and included in the final portfolio.

"When you and your students are clear about the criteria for selecting entries at the beginning of the portfolio process, the process tends to result in a fair, focused, and efficient assessment" (Rolheiser et al., 2000, p. 17). Since the portfolio selection process correlates so closely with the purpose and type of portfolio, only the items that achieve that purpose are included.

During the selection process, teachers will consider the array of formative assessment strategies that can be used to evaluate student performance. Since students participate as both self-evaluators and peer evaluators in the portfolio process, assessment strategies that build on the experiences and abilities of learners are recommended. These types of assessment are formative, ongoing, and placed in the hands of the students and teacher. It has been found that student involvement in assessment fosters more personal responsibility and motivation. Since peers are involved in performance assessment, artifact review, and even portfolio evaluation, assessment becomes collaborative, as well.

Other stakeholders such as parents, other teachers, and administrators can also play a part in the selection process of the portfolio. As students continuously apply the criteria of various assignments and performances, they begin to view assessment as a means for improving their learning. To this end, they seek out the views of peers, mentors, parents, and other stakeholders who use the same criteria to provide feedback to students. Students can then establish future goals to improve or strengthen the evidence of learning that will be shown through their portfolio artifact selections.

Subject or Content Area Learning—Just the Facts

Items that demonstrate what a student understands about a particular subject area (such as language arts, mathematics, science, or art) would be included in a subject or content area portfolio. Students and teachers work together to select the types of items that are representative of important concepts and skills in each subject area. A portfolio for a language arts class, for example, could contain book reports, key vocabulary words, a research paper, a response journal to a piece of literature, a letter to the editor, a poem, a panel discussion, a performance tape of a scene from a play, a reflection on the portfolio, a self-assessment, and a list of future goals. The teacher would engage students in decisions about the guidelines and the criteria for selecting items to include.

Learning Process—The Experience

In this type of portfolio, teachers and students select items that represent the unique learning process of each student. The content becomes a means to achieve an end, which promotes recognition of and celebration of multicultural differences. The portfolio focuses on students' skills and processes like speaking, listening, writing, reading, problem solving, decision making, higher-order thinking, and creativity. The students' proficiencies in these areas are demonstrated through written work, audio and video reproduction of performances, teacher observations, checklists, and interviews and conferences with students. (See Blacklines 4.5 and 4.6 at the end of this chapter.)

Multiple Intelligences—The Spectrum

The theory of multiple intelligences advanced by Gardner (1993) has been an adaptable match for academic portfolios. Several authors, including Chapman (1993), Fogarty and Stoehr (1995), and Jensen (2007) provide ideas for teachers for promoting students' awareness and understanding of the key ways in which they acquire knowledge and process information. Academic portfolios can help students showcase the ways in which "they are smart" by organizing entries around the eight intelligences. The student might include

- logs and journals to depict verbal/linguistic and intrapersonal intelligences;
- a Venn diagram to depict visual/spatial intelligence;
- a computer program to depict logical/mathematical intelligence;
- a video of a group performance to depict bodily/kinesthetic and interpersonal intelligences;
- a rap song or musical composition to represent musical/rhythmic intelligence; and
- a nature-walk analysis to represent naturalist intelligence.

The benefits of a multiple intelligence portfolio are far reaching. It not only stretches students to expand their repertoire of products and processes to meet academic goals, but it also provides acknowledgment and celebration of students' talents and special abilities, and encourages them to showcase them. Knowledge about multiple intelligences also promotes students' abilities to understand why they believe they are stronger in some areas and weaker in others. It often results in students' recognizing that they can improve in any subject if they know how they can improve if they set goals to do so.

Standards-Based—High Stakes

In a standards-based portfolio, all artifacts correlate to specific performance and content standards. Each entry has a standard listed on the top. Students sometimes fill out an entry sheet to describe the standard and complete a checklist or rubric to indicate academic achievement in each area. The dated entries show developmental growth over time.

Thematic Units or Projects—Dream Theme

The unit or thematic portfolio has always been a popular type of portfolio. Instead of including items from the entire quarter or semester, the portfolio is focused on a specific unit of study that can range from two to five weeks in length, with the portfolio containing 10 to 12 items. If the students study *ecology and the role of plants* for five weeks, they select entries that demonstrate their writing, reading, and speaking processes and their understanding of ecology.

For example, a thematic portfolio on ecology might include a poem about the rainforests, a Venn diagram comparing coniferous forests to rainforests, a video on a class field trip to the botanical garden, and drawings of plant structures. The teacher may require some categories that meet curriculum goals or standards, but the students often have a choice about the specific entries. (See the appendix for a sample portfolio.)

How Will the Items Be Selected?

Determining how the entries are to be selected is a key decision in the portfolio process. In a standards portfolio, for example, the entries must demonstrate a student's ability to meet learning goals and state standards. Sometimes the criteria and indicators for quality work are established by the teacher and the students in the classroom. Other times, many of these high-stakes assignments require the use of rubrics created by the district and state to ensure reliability and validity. (See Blacklines 4.5 and 4.7 at the end of this chapter.)

State Mandates—State's Stakes

State standards correlated to state tests and curriculum frameworks also determine criteria for selecting portfolio artifacts. In many instances, students and teachers can work together to translate state standards in subject areas or learning processes into student-friendly criteria for performances. Teachers may create student self-assessment forms and the artifact selection forms. In this way, the portfolio selection process ensures that content, goals, and evidence reflect clearly defined criteria that meet standards and benchmarks and help students perform well on state standardized tests. (See Examples 4.1 and 4.5 at the end of this chapter.)

Teacher- and Student-Created Criteria—It's Up to Us!

If the purpose of the portfolio is to review student work and set new goals, then the teacher and students develop the selection process. For example, the class votes to include representative work, but the students have some choice as to which items they include. They also create their own rubrics to assess the items according to criteria and indicators they determine. To help inform the selection process, see Figure 4.6 for a list of selection categories.

Who Will Select the Items?

Who are the stakeholders in the portfolio process? Who will participate in the selection of artifacts? Once again, the purpose of the portfolio determines who will select the items.

District- or State-Mandated Artifacts—It's the Law

If the portfolio is part of the formal assessment process for monitoring student achievement and teacher accountability, district or state educational leaders mandate which entries must be included. For example, a state might

Selection Categories

Media	**Group Work**	**Individual Work**
cassettes	projects	papers
slides	performances	tests
videos	peer reviews	journals
pictures	peer edits	logs
computer programs	social skills	homework
Processes	**Reflective**	**Multiple Intelligences**
biographies of works	self-assessments	logical/mathematical
rough drafts and	reflections	musical/rhythmic
final drafts	reflective journals	verbal/linguistic
sketches and final	artifact registries	bodily/kinesthetic
drawings	goal setting logs	visual/spatial
problem-solving	learning log	interpersonal
attempts		intrapersonal
		naturalist

Figure 4.6

require a biographical piece, a piece of creative writing, a résumé for a job, evidence of teamwork, an assignment that integrates two different subject areas, a problem and a solution, or a self-assessment. Some state departments of education determine the pieces that will be selected for inclusion in high-stakes portfolios. Each of these plays a major role in the evaluation process. The state usually provides a scoring guide or rubric to help teachers and students know the expectations of quality work and to compare students' work to the standards. The portfolio may be used in conjunction with grades, standardized test scores, and teacher recommendations to determine promotion or retention of students.

Student-Selected Artifacts—It's Up to Me!

Some teachers allow students to select all of the work they include in their portfolios. They recognize that students are the major stakeholders in the process and, therefore, should be responsible for their own learning. Some students select only their best work, while others include a few works in progress, some unsatisfactory pieces, and a few "not yets." Others highlight their lives outside of school and choose to select extracurricular, hobby, job-related, or community projects that reveal the whole student. Wiggins (1994) stresses that the selection process should be thoughtful and fun—but that it should also be challenging. (See Blacklines 4.8, 4.9, and 4.10 at the end of this chapter.)

Teacher-Selected Artifacts—I Have Goals

The teacher plays a critical role in the selection of portfolio pieces. The teacher's input ranges from obvious to subtle. The teacher makes choices to ensure that the items reflect school, district, or state requirements. These so-called high-stakes portfolios require certain entries. At other times, the teacher exercises the option to include any pieces that reflect the content or processes that represent the key concepts in the course. Teachers mix student-generated work with their own observations, quarterly or semester progress reports, scores on important standardized tests or teacher-made tests, anecdotal records, absentee records, or other items from the student's cumulative records. In this case, the confidentiality of the portfolio is paramount. These types of entries limit the access of portfolios because peers and other teachers would violate confidentiality issues by reviewing them.

Teacher- or Student-Selected Artifacts—Together Is Better

The teacher and student select artifacts that they both agree best meet the standards and criteria. Teachers plan for teacher/student selections to occur at natural intersections of teaching and learning, such as the completion of thematic units of study or at the end of each quarter or trimester. Often the teacher decides to include three or four items to meet content goals or district goals, and then allows students free choice on the rest of the selections.

Additionally, teachers assign categories—creative writing pieces, group projects, artwork, performances, media projects, reflections, logs, journals, a self-check observation list—but allow students the freedom to review their work and select their best entries in each category. This process allows the teacher to retain evidence of growth or achievement related to curriculum goals and standards while allowing students to retain their freedom of choice within the teacher's prescribed framework.

Peer-Selected Artifacts—All for One, One for All

Peer-selected artifacts involve the classroom community. Students intricately involved in the assessment process review the work of other students, offer constructive feedback, and help select pieces to include in another student's portfolio. For example, one student may believe a piece of artwork is not up to his usual standards and would rather not include it in his portfolio. A fellow student or the members of his group, however, may recognize qualities in the piece that make it worthy of entry into the portfolio. The peer can request that the student include the entry and can attach a commentary or reflection describing why he or she thinks the work is important.

Students in the peer-selection process listen empathetically, use encouraging words, and disagree with the idea—and not with the person. They assess the quality of work based on standards, criteria, and indicators included in the rubrics. The involvement of peers in the selection process encourages team building, trust building, and cooperation within the classroom community.

Parent-Selected Artifacts—Tell Me What You Think

Parents and significant others (caregivers or guardians, other teachers, counselors, siblings, principals, and school staff members) can play a vital role in the selection process. Students ask parents or others to review and select entries to include in their portfolios. This procedure helps parents become a part of the learning process and encourages students to discuss work with other people, not just the teacher. Parents can monitor students' progress throughout the quarter instead of just at the end. (See Example 4.7 at the end of this chapter.)

Teachers can provide parents or significant others with key questions to ask when making their selections. The parents or significant others write a reflection piece or commentary stating what they liked about the entry and why they thought it should or should not be included in the student's portfolio. (See Blackline 4.8 at the end of this chapter.)

When Will These Items Be Selected?

The what, how, and who aspects of the selection process are important. Another dimension to be considered is the when. Common occasions to make final selections for the portfolio are parent conferences, the end of a thematic unit, the end of a quarter, trimester, or semester, and the end of the year. Another option is to create a cumulative portfolio with work within a chosen time span.

Parent Conferences—Parent Talk

Portfolio reviews held during parent conferences provide valuable feedback for students, parents, and teachers. These portfolio conferences could take place during the end of any quarter or semester or at the end-of-year evaluation. The portfolio provides more concrete data than a grade book for communicating learner outcomes, student achievements, and student goals. Once again, parents review student work to ascertain their students' understanding of key concepts and attainment of important skills.

Examples

• • •

Performance Task Plan

Subject: Mathematics/Language Arts   Grade Level: 6

Curriculum: Making predictions from data

Standards:

1. Organize and display data using charts, circle graphs, bar graphs and double-line graph.

2. Make predictions and decisions based on data.

3. Write a persuasive letter.

Performance Task:

You have been asked by the owner of Acme Music Store to conduct a survey of 150 people of different age groups in our community to determine what type of music they would buy. Be prepared to present a circle graph representing percentages for responses; a bar graph depicting the relationship between the age groups; a double-line graphic for relationship between the gender and musical preference, and a prediction from your graphs about what inventory to stock.

Group Work:

One	Two	Three	Four
Write the survey Using categories such as rock, rap, country, classical, etc.	Construct a bar graph depicting the relationship between age groups and musical preference	Construct a double-line graphic showing the relationship between males and females and musical preference	Make a prediction from your graphs about what inventory to stock

Individual Work Correlated to Standards:

1. Write a persuasive letter to the new owner of Acme Music convincing her to stock music that the community would be willing to buy.

2. Use six categories (rock, rap, country, classical, blue, etc.); design a circle graph poster, representing responses from the people interviewed.

Methods of Assessment:

1. Checklist to assess each group's work.

2. Rubric to assess the persuasive letter.

3. Checklist to assess individual circle graphs.

Example 4.1

Storage

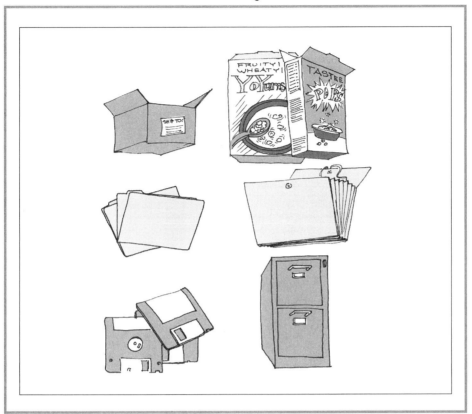

Example 4.2

Organizational Flow

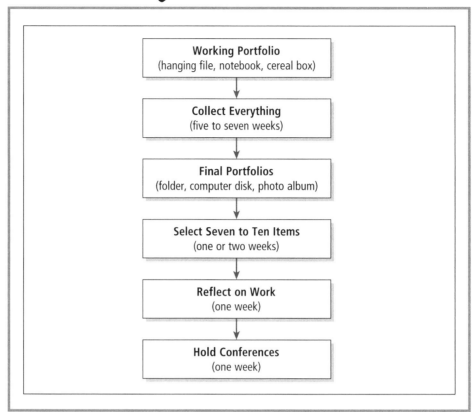

Example 4.3

Organizational Tools

ARTIFACT REGISTRY

Name *Mary S.*   Class *American Literature*

DELETIONS

Date	Item	Reasons for Deleting
4/18/01	Book report on *The Great Gatsby*	I didn't understand symbolism so I used Spark Notes. Not my best work.
4/30/01	Sonnet on Sylvia Plath	I was so worried about a rhyme scheme that content suffered.

ADDITIONS

Date	Item	Reasons for Adding
4/18/01	Book report on *Tender Is the Night*	I liked this book by Fitzgerald better. I could figure out symbolism on my own.
4/30/01	Free verse poem on Plath	It didn't rhyme, but I said what I felt. More meaningful.

BIOGRAPHY OF A WORK LOG

Assignment: *Present a Decade in History*

Date	Log Entry
5/2/01	Group voted to pick the decade of the 1920s for presentation.
5/3/01	Brainstormed ideas for key elements of decade.
5/7/01	Went to media center to research key elements.
5/8/01	Divided key elements among five members: (1) historical events (4) music (2) politics (5) art (3) clothes
5/9–5/16/01	Gathered information, costumes, music, artifacts, newspaper headlines.
5/17–5/23/01	Wrote script for skit, made slides, selected music.
5/24/01	Presented retrospect of 1920s to the class.

Comments: The group worked well together. We learned the Charleston!

Example 4.4

Standards and Performance Tasks

BIOLOGY

Standard: Students will investigate the diversity of organisms by exploring diverse environments.

Performance Task:

Your team will be sent on a survival training mission to a remote biome. You need to research your biome and prepare your team to survive for six weeks. Prepare a map of the area, graphs of rainfalls and temperatures, an analysis of food available, and a chart of plants and animals indigenous to the area. You will present your data to the new recruits on _October 8_ .

MATHEMATICS

Standards: Operatives and procedures, measurement, statistics, and probability

Objective: Geometry operations

The city council has selected our class to bid on the landscaping design of a new garden for the town square. The project will include a scale drawing of the design, a cost estimation, a time line, a presentation to the city council, and an official proposal and contract. Be prepared to present your proposal at the City Council Board meeting on _December 17_.

SOCIAL STUDIES

Standard: Students will understand election processes and responsibilities of citizens.

Objective: Debate the electoral college

Your class has been selected to debate a class at a rival school on the local television station. You must defend the electoral college process. In preparation for your debate, you must research the electoral college, prepare both pro and con arguments, practice debate rules and strategies, and prepare 4″ × 6″ note cards with key arguments. The debate is scheduled for _February 19_.

Example 4.5

Checklist of Kindergarten Student Learning: Mathematics

Kindergarten: Students will correctly name simple two- and three-dimensional figures and recognize them in the environment

Performance Indicators: The students will	Not Taught	Taught (Date)
Recognize Two-Dimensional Shapes		
• Triangles		
• Rectangles		
• Squares		
• Circles		
Name Two-Dimensional Shapes		
• Triangles		
• Rectangles		
• Squares		
• Circles		
Recognize Three-Dimensional Shapes		
• Spheres (balls)		
• Cubes		
Name Three-Dimensional Shapes		
• Spheres (balls)		
• Cubes		
Observe Concrete Objects in Environment		
• Houses, schools, churches, driveways		
• Swimming pools, sports balls		
• Plants, playgrounds, landscaping		

Example 4.6

Dear Mom and Dad

Dear Mom and Dad:

In my social studies working folder you will see the work I have completed this term. I need your help in selecting best work that meets standards. Each of the three pieces my teacher and I placed in the folder have the rubric and comment sheet attached. You will see what I was expected to do and what I accomplished. Please use the checklist below to select your favorite piece.

Love,

Evan

Parent-Selected Portfolio Artifact

Student Name: Evan P.   Subject: Social Studies

Grade Level: Five   Term: Fall   Date: November 4, 2006

Checklist for Selection of Best Work Artifact

Parents: Please look at each piece in your student's folder. Select the one that you feel represents his or her best achievement, and complete the checklist below and place back in your student's working folder.

Artifact	Yes	No
1. The work shown by the piece meets the standards indicated in the rubric and shows the student completed it by the due date.	X	
2. The work shows progress in accomplishment of the learning standard.	X	
3. The work is completed with few mechanical errors.	X	
4. The work is impressive.	X	

Comments:

Dear Evan,

We think your piece showing your understanding of the way in which the Native Americans responded to the Westward Expansion is well done. Your work shows that you met all the points and your reflection shows that you understand how any people would feel when their land and culture are taken away from them. Very impressive. We are proud of your work!

Love,

Mom and Dad

Example 4.7

Blacklines

Portfolio Organizational Flow

Collect Items for Working Portfolios

Dates: _____

Select Items for Final Portfolio

Dates: _____

Describe and Reflect on All Items

Dates: _____

Conference With Peers and Teacher

Dates: _____

Blackline 4.1

Portfolio Entry

Standard:

Title or Description of Entry: _____
_____
_____

Personal Reflection: _____
_____
_____
_____

Student: _____ Grade: _____ Date: _____

- -

Portfolio Entry

Standard:

Title or Description of Entry: _____
_____
_____

Personal Reflection: _____
_____
_____
_____

Student: _____ Grade: _____ Date: _____

Blackline 4.2

Artifact Registry

Student _____ Class _____

DELETIONS

Date	Item	Reasons for Deleting

ADDITIONS

Date	Item	Reasons for Adding

Blackline 4.3

Biography of a Work Log

Assignment: _____

Standard: _____

Date	Log Entry

Comments:

Signed: _____

Date: _____

Blackline 4.4

Performance Task Plan

Subject: _____ Grade Level: _____

Curriculum: _____

Standards:

Performance Task:

Group Work:

  one   two   three   four   five

Individual Work Correlated to Standards:

1.

2.

3.

4.

Methods of Assessment:

Blackline 4.5

Multiple Intelligences Portfolio

Unit: _____ Time Frame: _____ Grade/Subject: _____

Standards: (1) _____

(2) _____

(3) _____

Verbal/Linguistic	Logical/Mathematical	Visual/Spatial	Bodily/Kinesthetic
Musical/Rhythmic	Interpersonal	Intrapersonal	Naturalist

Standards Pieces	Item 1	Item 2	Item 3	Item 4
Student Choice	Item 5	Item 6	Item 7	Item 8

Blackline 4.6

Performance Task Checklist

Standard: _____

Assignment: _____

Create a cluster checklist for the Individual Work Assignment in your performance task.

Criteria/Performance Indicators	Not Yet 0	Some Evidence 1
•		
•		
•		
•		
•		
•		
•		
•		
•		
•		
•		
•		
•		
•		
•		
•		
•		
•		
Comments		

Blackline 4.7

My Reflection on Strengths and Challenges

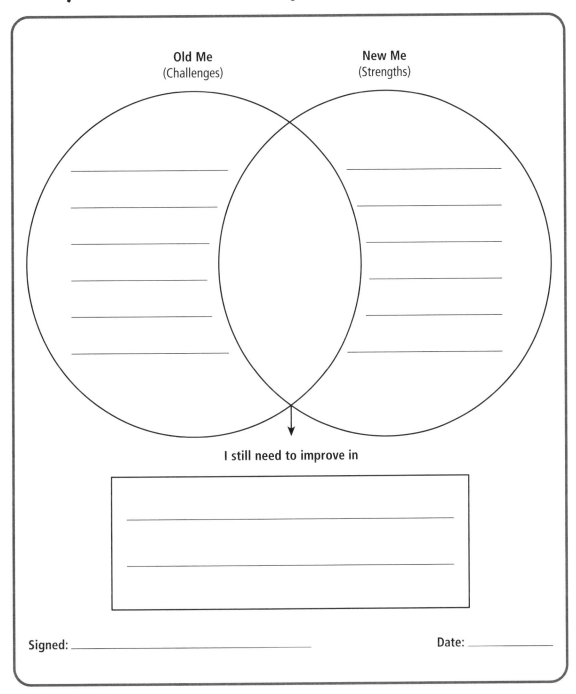

Old Me
(Challenges)

New Me
(Strengths)

I still need to improve in

Signed: _____   Date: _____

Blackline 4.8

My Reflection on Goal Setting

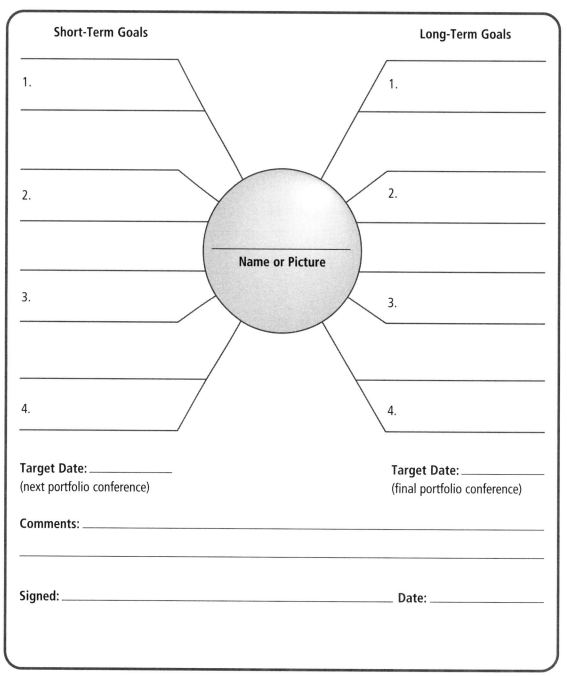

Short-Term Goals

1.

2.

3.

4.

Long-Term Goals

1.

2.

3.

4.

Name or Picture

Target Date: _____
(next portfolio conference)

Target Date: _____
(final portfolio conference)

Comments: _____

_____

Signed: _____ **Date:** _____

Blackline 4.9

Possible Selection for Final Portfolio

Use the following chart to organize and plan selections for the final portfolio. The teacher should select the required pieces first and then tell the students to select entries they feel showcase their best work.

Teacher—Standard

Student Pick—Standard

Teacher—Standard

Student Pick—Free Choice

Teacher—Curriculum Goal

Student Self-Assessment

Peer/Parent Pick

Student Reflection

Student Pick—Standard

Student Goal Setting

Blackline 4.10

Connect Students' Reflections and Self-Assessments to Criteria, Rubrics, and Standards

OVERVIEW

Ensuring success in the use of academic portfolios requires that educators know how to engage students in reflection, self-assessment, and goal setting at the *beginning, middle,* and *end* of the portfolio assessment process. As we have asserted throughout this book, teachers need to develop their knowledge of how to use authentic assessments to focus on students' ability to produce quality products and performances. Portfolios will place students at the heart of assessment as reviewers, critics, and evaluators of their work—as well as the work of their peers. Therefore, connecting students' voices in the ongoing assessment and evaluation of their own work needs to be seen as an important part of daily activities. Students who develop the ability to inspect their own work will also develop the ability to self-monitor and set academic achievement goals.

INTRODUCTION

Self-evaluation is an important part of the cognitive function psychologists (Costa, 2006; Flavell, 1976; Schoenfeld, 1987) have termed *metacognition*. This ability to think about one's thinking or develop knowledge of one's own thoughts and the factors that influence one's own thinking occur when students are regularly encouraged to make judgments about their achievements and then to reflect on these judgments.

The *portfolio selection process* requires that students continuously review their collection of artifacts. When given time and authentic assessment tools to match their work with predetermined criteria, review their overall strengths and weaknesses, make adjustments, and determine future directions, students develop lifelong learning skills that will serve them as individual workers and team members. In essence, they will develop their metacognitive thinking abilities.

THE BEGINNING—TOOLS THAT PROMOTE STUDENTS' REFLECTION AND SELF-ASSESSMENT

To promote success with student self-assessment and goal setting, teachers need to introduce students early in the year to the authentic assessment tools that engage them in metacognitive processes. By providing guided practice in the introduction of learning logs and pictorial lists, checklists, and scoring rubrics across all subject areas, teachers can ensure that students will become accurate and reflective participants in their own learning and assessment. Within the portfolio process, the principal purpose of using these assessment tools is to assist students in achieving ownership, responsibility, and a true sense of voice. This accomplishment will pay off as students become engaged in planning the direction of their learning journeys and become more involved with planning how their goals will be accomplished. Whether teachers use a paper portfolio or an e-portfolio, these tools will serve as the key support for students' reflection and selection of the clear and compelling evidence showing attainment of the portfolio's purpose.

Learning logs and lists, reflective journals, pictorial lists, and analyses of strengths and challenges are the most appropriate tools for reflective student inspection. The process of inspection helps students to know if they are on track to meet standards or other portfolio purposes. They can be used as catalysts for setting new goals, strategies, or directions. These simple tools are often used in conjunction with language arts and English curricula because they introduce students to effective ways to self-monitor their work and progress. However, they can be used across all subjects in the curriculum as they engage students in the habits of mind of striving for accuracy, metacognition, thinking, persistence, communicating with clarity and precision, and applying past knowledge to new situations.

Establishing Criteria—What Is Important

In the beginning of the portfolio or e-portfolio process, students need to look at each individual piece of their work and react to it. In this stage, students acquire the knowledge and dispositions to confidently assess their work according to known criteria. It is helpful if teachers engage students in listing criteria they think are important for achieving or surpassing goals on assignments, performances, and projects. Teachers can do this in the early primary grades or with special needs students by using learning lists and logs with very simple criteria. Later, in the intermediate grades and up, students will become more skillful in identifying criteria and working with their teachers in establishing checklists and scoring rubrics. (See Example 5.1 at the end of this chapter.)

Learning Logs—Log Your Reflections

Learning logs are the simplest of assessment tools for promoting student self-reflection. "Logs usually consist of short, more objective entries that contain mathematics, problem solving entries, observations of science experiments, questions about the lecture or reading, lists of outside readings, homework assignments, or anything that lends itself to keeping records" (Burke, 2005, p. 120). Logs provide succinct record keeping across the curriculum and contain basic criteria that that make them ideal for students with special needs. For example, a first-grade class might develop learning lists that start, "One thing I am working on in my reading is . . ." or "My best work in math is . . ." Learning logs can then be geared to criteria that are useful throughout both the elementary and secondary levels of school.

Learning Lists—First, Second, Third . . .

Learning lists are often loose-leaf papers for traditional portfolios or one-page stems provided for online e-portfolios. They also include stem statements that trigger students' thinking about attributes or objectives within the learning process. Learning lists enable even the youngest of students and students with special needs to think backward and record their thoughts about their work. While doing this they note achievements, difficulties, and goals, and acknowledge or celebrate them.

Teachers of early primary children or students with special needs who are not yet literate often interview children by using learning lists. When teachers use them regularly, students become accustomed to looking backward and valuing the work they have done as they assess their progress toward a goal. Figure 5.1 shows an example of a first-grade learning list in mathematics. (See Example 5.2 and Blackline 5.1 at the end of this chapter.)

Sometimes teachers of older students will interview them about revisions or additions to learning lists. As teachers gain experience they will know how to vary "stem statements" that are great tools for triggering students' thinking about what they have learned and what they want to learn.

Stem statements include, "New things I have learned are . . .", "One thing I'm having trouble with is . . .", or "Some stories I have written are. . . ." As Figure 5.2 shows, learning logs help students focus more critically on their learning by writing about what they have learned and by thinking about knowledge, skills, or concepts that are difficult for them to acquire. (See Example 5.3 at the end of this chapter.)

My Math Learning List

Name: David Brown

My best work in math is

One thing I want to remember is

One goal I have is

Figure 5.1

Learning Log for Spanish

Name: Cathy Grant

One thing I am doing well: *I am working on my pronunciation in the lab every chance I can get.*

One thing I have trouble with: *There are so many tenses and forms of verbs. I always get confused!*

One goal I have: *By the end of the term I want to earn a "B" on my fluency.*

Figure 5.2

Creating Checklists—Checking Them Twice

Because they assist students in self-assessment and peer assessment, checklists have become frequently used tools for observational and anecdotal assessment. Students can use checklists themselves to evaluate their progress in work habits, study skills, and organizational skills. Checklists can be developed by teachers when they want to transfer the language of district or state standards into comprehensible learning criteria or targets for students. Checklists are ways for teachers to effectively generate their own criteria to guide both teaching and learning. For example, if teachers need to make sure that students understand all the qualities that must be integrated in an oral presentation, they can engage students in discussing what a good oral presentation sounds like. After brainstorming and discussing the criteria they have established, the students will understand completely what will be expected from their performances (Figure 5.3).

Criteria for an Oral Performance

Secondary Level

1. Voice
   - Expression
   - Tone
   - Feeling

2. Volume

3. Enunciation

4. Content
   - Facts
   - Quotes
   - Statistics

Figure 5.3

Another way in which checklists can be used is in promoting a sense of accomplishment in staying with a task. In order to become effective learners, students need to know how to reflect on their social skills and intelligent behaviors, such as persistence, checking for accuracy, and insightfulness (Costa & Kallick, 1992, 1995, 2000). Toward this end, many teachers use checklists to collect data on how students are learning or acquiring knowledge, skills, and dispositions. Teachers have recently begun to recognize the importance of having students themselves use and apply the information gained from checklists of behaviors—just as they do for subject area tasks. Students from the primary grades through high school, including special needs students, can benefit from applying criteria of the characteristics of social skills and then identifying their strengths and weaknesses. This again promotes student voice in setting goals for improvement. By learning how to monitor their own behavior, products, work habits, and thinking skills, as well as learning how to monitor the behavior and products of their peers, students can become self-regulating, autonomous learners who take initiative in their own education. (See Example 5.5 at the end of this chapter.)

Persevering to accomplish a difficult problem is a good example of how students can be engaged in developing the criteria for checklists. Teachers ask students to identify the qualities of a persistent person. By using an authentic assessment tool called a "T-chart," the ideas elicited from the students can later be used to establish the known criteria. These in turn are used as guidelines or indicators of student progress. Burke (2005) describes T-charts as tools that help, "students understand what certain behaviors 'look like' and 'sound like.'" (See Blackline 5.3 at the end of this chapter.)

Teachers will direct students to staple their checklists to completed assignments that will go in a working folder. Later, the use of these basic assessment tools will provide the concrete information or evidence needed to show student progress in the portfolio or e-portfolio. (See Blackline 5.4 at the end of this chapter.)

T-chart on Persistence—Intermediate/Middle Grade Levels

Looks Like	Sounds Like
Checks work over and over.	I can do this.
Writes several drafts.	I will write it again.
Tries task over and over.	I will try it again.
Uses different ways to solve a problem.	There has to be another way to solve this problem.
Stays with a task even when frustrated.	I am not going to give up yet.

Figure 5.4

Self-Assessment Checklist for Intelligent Behaviors—Middle Grades

Criterion-Persistence	Yes	No
Indicators:		
1. I know how to access information.	x	
2. I try several approaches.		x
3. I do not give up quickly.		x
4. I have patience.		
5. I brainstorm alternative solutions.	x	
6. I check my own work.		x
7. I write several drafts.		x
8. I problem solve.	x	

Figure 5.5

SCORING RUBRICS

Rubrics are useful tools for choosing criteria students must meet and for using the resulting rubric to assess student work. Familiarizing students with rubrics is an important first step in using portfolios or e-portfolios as containers of evidence. Teachers can introduce rubrics to students by creating a "fun rubric" on something that is age appropriate (and school appropriate), and with which the students are familiar.

For primary-age children, a rubric can be created around the topic of a birthday party; for intermediate grade students, a rubric can be created around a topic such as a party, a movie, pizza, and recess or school lunch. (See Example 5.7 at the end of this chapter.) Secondary-level students will enjoy creating a fun rubric around topics such as a school dance, football or soccer game, a music concert, or prom.

The activity shown in Figure 5.6 illustrates a typical outcome of a rubric for a birthday party. It is led by placing students in groups of five, asking them to select the fun topic to assess, and then having them develop criteria and indicators related to these criteria. It will take the students as little as 25 minutes to create their own fun rubric on easel paper. When the students share their fun rubrics and talk about the process of writing rubrics, they will be internalizing the importance of criteria to determine degrees of quality. (See Blacklines 5.3 and 5.5 at the end of this chapter.)

"Once students have become familiar with the format of a performance rubric, they will be better able to understand how to use this rubric to assess their products, tasks and performances" (Burke, 2005, p. 86). For example, students can be led to take the criteria that were determined for the checklist on persistence and further develop them as a performance rubric. Figure 5.7 shows the results of this transformation, and Figure 5.8 illustrates the use of a performance rubric at the middle school level.

A variation of the scoring rubric used for performances of primary and special needs students is the pictorial reflective rubric. The example in Figure 5.9 has been used by Alaska teachers in the primary grades, and can be adapted for students with special needs. (See Blackline 5.2 at the end of this chapter.)

Creating a Fun Rubric

1. Line up according to the month and date of your birthday.

2. Call out your birthday and section off in groups of five according to month and then day, if needed.

3. Roles in each group:
   - Earliest birthday: Organizer
   - Second-earliest birthday: Materials manager (newsprint and markers)
   - Third-earliest birthday: Recorder (write)
   - Fourth-earliest birthday: Reporter (share)
   - Last birthday: Encourager ("Awesome," and help other group members)

4. Task: Select a fun topic and create a rubric to assess it.

5. Time limit: 25 minutes

6. Sharing: Reporter shares rubric

7. Processing: Value of doing a fun rubric

Figure 5.6

Performance Rubric on Persistence

Criterion: Persistence	Not Yet	Seldom	Sometimes	Most of the Time
Indicators:				
1. I know how to access information.	x			
2. I try several approaches.		x		
3. I do not give up quickly.		x		
4. I have patience.				x
5. I brainstorm alternative solutions.	x			
6. I check my own work.		x		
7. I write several drafts.		x		
8. I problem solve.			x	

Figure 5.7

Self-Assessment Checklist for a Research Paper in Middle School

Criterion: Research on the Prairies	Not Yet	Almost There	Got It
Indicators:			
1. I know how to access print information.	x		x
2. I look up several print sources.			x
3. I know how to access electronic information.		x	
4. I know how to record information.			x
5. I know how to cite sources accurately.	x		
6. I know how to write the bibliography of sources.		x	
7. Use the information from my sources to support my point.		x	

Figure 5.8

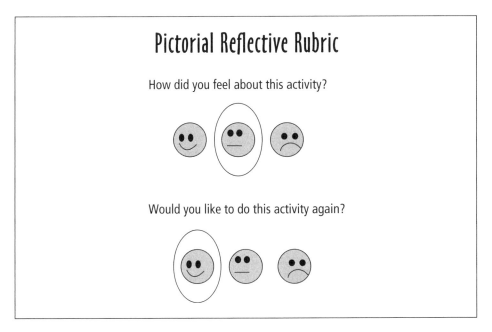

Figure 5.9

When teachers use performance tasks in which students have been involved in creating criteria, checklists, and rubrics, those teachers are better prepared to design portfolios and e-portfolios that contain evidence of students' learning experiences. These "artifacts" are then used to show alignment with the portfolios' purposes or content standards. In addition, the engagement of students in these authentic assessment tasks helps them to achieve "voice" in representing as well as showcasing their school work on communication processes, problem solving, accessing information, creativity, and many other areas of their education.

PLANNING TO IMPLEMENT E-PORTFOLIOS

When choosing to use a digital platform to create e-portfolios, it is important that considerable time be spent on the selection of the tools that will be used to manage the e-portfolio. Depending on the available school or classroom computer platforms (Apple or Microsoft), a variety of tools will need to be selected. The principal criteria for selection of these tools should be that they allow students to easily save their artifacts and "publish" their portfolios. This "publication" will likely be on USB drives, CDs, or a local area network server (LAN). If the school has a district Web page, then it is possible for students to use very basic software such as *Hyperstudio* or Microsoft Office's *Word* or *FrontPage.* Student at the middle grades are often able to use the Microsoft software to become developers of their own e-portfolios. Younger students can use basic forms of word processing or *Hyperstudio.* High school students are often capable of using the *Dreamweaver* Web publishing software that provides a more professional look for the e-portfolio. Portfolio developers need to ensure the confidentiality and security of any identifying materials students may post on the district's Internet location.

THE MIDDLE—TOOLS THAT PROMOTE STUDENTS' REFLECTION AND SELF-ASSESSMENT WITH PEERS

Following the forming and norming of students' understanding of the performance assessments covered previously, it becomes important to assist them in becoming "critical friends" to their peers. This is often begun as early as kindergarten when teachers invite students to participate in "author's chair," literature and writing circles, and small group portfolio sharing. Figure 5.10 is an example from a kindergarten peer reflection.

Kindergarten Peer Reflection

Author's Chair: Kind Compliments

Name: Christopher

One thing I liked about your story: *Your dog is funny.*

You did a good job on *the picture of your dog*

Signed

Ivan

Figure 5.10

As middle school students gain the intrapersonal ability to reflect on their learning, and as they develop their social skills and habits of mind, teachers can begin to connect students to the work of their peers. Teachers in the United Kingdom have been using peer assessment for a key reason: "By judging the work of others, students gain insight into their own performance" (Bostock, 2006). Figure 5.11 presents some middle school to high school examples that demonstrate how peer assessment leads to self-assessment. (See Example 5.8 at the end of this chapter.)

In the cooperative learning classroom, it is well recognized that becoming interdependent and responsible group members enhances learning and assessment (Bellanca & Fogarty, 1994; Stiggins, 1994, 2002). David Johnson and Roger Johnson (1994, 1996, 2007) assert that "student involvement increases the possibility for more diverse outcomes as well as the additional sources of labor to conduct assessments and communicate results" (p. 1). Teachers can engage students in peer reflection when they provide them with many opportunities to provide "kind compliments" for peer performances and products, or complete checklists of group performances, products, and projects. In the early grades, it is often beneficial to students to give them the cooperative role of "observer" where they move about the room during a group task and tally the times they observe selected social skills, habits of mind, and learning outcomes accomplished by peers (Figure 5.12). This often helps them to appreciate the outcomes of successful group sharing and cooperation while also providing models of effective social skills.

Peer Review of Student Work—Middle School and High School

Student Name: Taleen

Date: December 1, 2006

Subject: Social Studies

Strengths of this piece of work: *Your artwork on the map is so pretty! I think you deserve an A on the whole assignment!*

Weaknesses of this piece of work: *There are none. It is great!*

How the captions could be improved: *You could use a darker color for your captions but they are spelled correctly.*

On the rubric I would rate it as: *It's an A!*

What I would have to do to turn this into a grade project: *Just change the colors of the captions.*

Some other suggestions I have for you: *Keep up the great artistic work!*

What it helps me think of for adding or changing my own project: *I think that I would like to work harder on my own drawing and do a couple drafts before my finished product.*

Janelle

Peer Reviewer

Figure 5.11

Social Skills Rubric

Student Name: Aracelli	Not Yet	Almost	Got It!
Stayed in your group			x
Used your "6" voice	x		
Helped your group complete the task on time		x	
Encouraged other students		x	

Figure 5.12

Promoting peer review in literature circles and writing circles for older students is also recognized as a positive source of student learning and confidence in the development of reading and writing processes. A number of assessment tools can be successfully used to promote peer assessment in these and similar peer activities. Among them are "kind compliments," group-work self-assessment checklists ("rate your mates"), observation checklists for peer evaluations and self-evaluations, peer questions for reflective feedback, and peer problem-solving rating scales. (See Blackline 5.8 at the end of this chapter.)

The state of Alaska maintains a Web page regarding peer evaluation that is provided to teachers of mathematics. Among the key ideas it suggests are the following (Alaska Department of Education and Early Development, 1996, Section F):

It is common for students to have difficulty when they are first asked to report their feelings, beliefs, intentions, or thinking processes. It is even more difficult to report on their peers' performance. Make the process safer by using it for formative rather than summative purposes.

Model evaluating your own performance, or provide examples. Another strategy is to introduce constructive feedback. Models help students develop their sense of standards for their own performance.

Work on constructive feedback between students. Do a lot of modeling first, and then make one positive statement and one area for improvement. The students then will pick another classmate to make a positive and an improvement comment as well.

Let students do a private self-assessment that no one else sees. This allows for an honest sense of their own level of understanding and performance.

Self-assessment and peer assessment can sometimes be combined onto one checklist format; however, one set of responses may influence the other.

Similarly, the Saskatchewan Ministry of Education (2007) posts a sample peer assessment as an important part of the overall student evaluation process on its Web site. Educators are encouraged to use peer assessment "particularly when there is a product, presentation or project. . . . Students can assess other

Alaska Reflective Feedback and Problem-Solving Checklist

Criteria	stu 1	stu 2
Collaborates with others	⦙	
States problems in own words	⦙	⦙
Solves problems in more than one way	⦙	⦙

Figure 5.13

groups and members of their own group. Even at grade one, where one might do three stars (good points) and a wish (for next time), students can be objective and produce reasons for their ratings" (p. xx). (See Blackline 5.7 at the end of this chapter.)

The high school teacher will also find that students place more effort and quality into their work when they know that their work will be evaluated not only by the teacher but also by one or more peers. Peer assessment ensures that not only subject area knowledge but also social skills and intelligent behaviors are to be assessed. Students often respond by putting their best efforts into the product, presentation, or project.

"Rate Your Mate" Secondary Peer Assessment

Please use the following criteria to assess your partner or team member's contribution to the task.

Evaluating My Partner/Team Member NAME:	1	2	3
Motivation	prevented me from doing my work.	helped me do better	motivated and encouraged me the entire way.
Work	did very little	helped the group a little.	group worked well because of member's efforts
Contribution	work quality suffered because member did not help	helped at times.	did all of the expected work to the best of member's ability.

Student comments:

Teacher comments:

Figure 5.14

THE ROLE OF THE WORKING PORTFOLIO SELECTION PROCESS

Whether or not they know it as such, most teachers train their students to maintain a working portfolio folder. Better known as the "working folder," this is the day-to-day container that holds students' work-in-progress, completed work that is destined to become part of the portfolio, or pieces of work that are somehow significant to a student's progress or achievement. It is not uncommon for the working folder to become overcrowded with teacher-selected, student-selected, and even peer-selected pieces, which is why regular or periodic review of the folder is such an important part of the portfolio process.

During the middle phase of the portfolio process (as has been described earlier), students learn how to reflect on established criteria, establish performance goals, complete a piece of work or performance, and then self-assess or evaluate the outcome using the established scoring rubric. The achievement of these processes—reflection, goal setting, and self-assessment—become key to the portfolio selection process that occurs now.

When students are regularly invited to review the content of their working folders while using criteria and scoring tools that have been previously discussed, they once again obtain voice in the assessment process. The "selective abandonment" that will be needed for each student to scan all the pieces held in the working folder and compare them to the criteria of best achievement becomes central to this stage of the portfolio process. And this, of course, is why teachers have engaged students in the acquisition of these skills and dispositions throughout the period leading up to portfolio selection. (See Example 5.6 at the end of this chapter.)

Checklists and rubrics once again become the tools that assist teachers and their students in developing portfolios or e-portfolios that are authentic representations of students' achievements and learning dispositions. These tools are used in combination with various student conferences. For example, in primary grades or with special needs students, teachers might regularly sit down with students to go through the work that has accumulated in the working folder. (See Example 5.9 at the end of this chapter.) Knowing that "less is more," teachers encourage students to select pieces that best show who they are as readers, writers, problem solvers, decision makers, and so on, and then examine the scoring rubrics that accompany the pieces. This results in selections for the portfolio that represent how the students have met the learning objectives or goals.

Similarly, peer conferences are often held as students "look at their work together" in order to select the most appropriate pieces for the portfolio. During this time, the students become reacquainted with earlier standards or criteria for achievement and come to value the opportunity and outcome of looking at significant pieces of work that can represent them in their portfolios. Following are some of the selection tools that teachers provide to students at this important point in the portfolio process.

THE CULMINATION—DEEPENING STUDENTS' REFLECTION AND SELF-ASSESSMENT ON THE FINAL PORTFOLIO

The best research on cognitive development suggests that it is extremely important for students to think about their own thinking, and to reflect on how they learn and why they fail to learn (Mills-Courts & Amiran, 1991). When people use metacognition they can "describe the steps and sequences used before, during, and after problem solving" (Costa, 1991, p. 23). Student voice is strengthened when portfolio and e-portfolio processes invite peers and parents to participate in joint review and acknowledgment of each student's achievements. The interdependence that was created throughout the earlier assessment stages of the portfolio process is extended and deepened at the conclusion.

Teachers will find that students achieve greater satisfaction and meaning in their work as they sit beside one another to share new insights and offer compliments and suggestions to their peers. Parents find a meaningful and engaging opportunity to learn about and value their child's achievement, and to join with their child to set new goals.

Reflection logs, journals, and checklists that have been created by teachers earlier in the process will now help students self-assess how well they have met their academic goals. The last step for using checklists in the portfolio process is for students' inspection of the portfolio or e-portfolio. A Portfolio Inspection Checklist (Figure 5.15) references the technical requirements for the final portfolio. When used in the portfolio process, the checklist delineates the overall goals of the portfolio or e-portfolio. More specifically, the checklist references particular standards or portfolio goals that have been targeted for the project. This "inspecting phase" is the time for an informal self-evaluation, or a check of the overall direction desired by the student. It is the opportunity to ask questions about the next steps along the chosen or changing pathway. It is the moment of truth that signals to learners whether or not they are on track, what measures they might need to take to realign their aims and goals, or if setting new goals may lead them in an entirely different direction. Here is an important opportunity for the teacher to enter into dialogue with the student—the intersection where the student seeks guidance and advice on achieving the set goals or desired outcomes. (See Blackline 5.11 at the end of this chapter.)

Sample Portfolio Inspection Checklist

Goals	YES	NO
1. Integrate technology into the biology project.		
2. Learn about a genetic disease.		
3. Demonstrate a personal pedigree.		
Standards		
1. Show evidence of the writing process.		
2. Demonstrate understanding of the concept of inherited traits.		
Requirements		
1. Include ten items in portfolio.		
2. Reflect on each item.		
3. Add a table of contents.		
4. Complete the project on time.		
5. Share my portfolio with a partner.		

Figure 5.15

To Grade or Not to Grade

The question of whether to grade students' final portfolios requires reflection and careful consideration. Once again, the purpose of the portfolio must be reviewed in order to align the portfolio outcome with its stated purpose. If the portfolio is developmental or best work, for example, it will not provide added value to grade the portfolio. Since it is likely that the pieces found in this type of portfolio were graded earlier, it is more important at this point that the student self-assess growth or evaluate how this piece showcases best work or significant development.

If the portfolio purpose is to show evidence of meeting standards, some items included in this type of portfolio—such as tests and term papers—would have been graded on original submission. Other assignments that are not subjective, such as mathematics problems, are usually given a grade at the time the learning occurs. Nevertheless, some teachers and parents—and even students—believe that grades in the final portfolio give students a goal to work toward. When deciding to grade items after they are placed in a final portfolio, teachers must determine ahead of time how they are to be graded. There are several methods to choose from if this meets the purposes of the portfolio or e-portfolio.

Previously Graded Entries—What Did I Get?

Many standards portfolios contain a selection of items that may have been previously graded. The items have been turned in earlier in the quarter and assessed according to grading standards established by the district, teacher, or students. Sometimes the grading is done with *rubrics*—guidelines for giving scores based on performance criteria and a rating scale. For example, if students receive a grade for creating a graph in mathematics, that grade would be in the grade book, but the rubric could be attached to the graph. (See Figure 5.16 and Blacklines 5.9 and 5.10 at the end of this chapter.)

Since all the work in this type of portfolio has already been graded, the portfolio is used for students to review their work, to trace growth and development. Often, when it comes time to conduct portfolio conferences, students are encouraged to revise and refine their previously graded work to improve the quality of their entries before sharing the portfolio with others. They can staple both copies together to show the corrections they have made and include the original rubric to show whether they met standards. The reflective comments that students add to these artifacts in the final portfolio or e-portfolio will reveal students' intrapersonal feelings and the goals they have set for future growth.

Key Items Selected for Grading—Roulette Wheel

Sometimes teachers will tell students in advance which entries will be graded after the portfolio is submitted. Teachers might select two items that they believe are important (e.g., research paper, cooperative project, or oral presentation) and then allow students to self-select two or three other items to be graded. This method allows teachers to make sure key accountability pieces are included, while also promoting student voice in encouraging students to

Grade 8 Rubric for Algebra Data Analysis Using Inequalities

Illinois State Math Goal 8: Use algebraic and analytical methods to identify and describe patterns and relationships in data, solve problems, and predict results.

Task Description: The music store you work for has asked you to recommend what kind of music it should order for next month. It needs information on what types of music are preferred by different age groups (under 10 yrs., teens, adults). You are to take a survey, display your results in a chart, include three types of graphs (triple bar, stem and leaf, and box and whisker plot), and write up a recommendation for your boss after you analyze the data.

Criteria	Indicators	0–1 Not Yet	2 Almost	3 Meets Expectations	4 Exceeds Expectations	Score
Format	• Has name, class period on cover • Turned in on time	• No name or class period on cover • Not on time	• Has name, class period on cover • Turned in time	NA	NA	
Web page	• Color title • Related graphics • Working links • Sources cited	Text only, 3–4 errors, incomplete footer and sources	Title, 2–3 errors, unrelated graphic, some sources cited	Title with color graphics, easy to read, 0–1 errors, all links work, sources cited	Superior attractive design that enhances topic, creative links, sources properly cited	
Overheads	• Colorful title slide includes graphs • Readable, no errors • Bibliography	Title page, no graphics, more than 3 errors, inaccurate graphs, and no bibliography	Title, some graphics, 2–3 errors, inaccurate graphs and bibliography	Title, graphics, graphs, 0–1 errors, bibliography	Creative title, appropriate graphics, accurate graphs, no errors, bibliography	
Graphs	• Break-even equation • Profit equation • Line graphs	Correct or partially correct display of only 1 of 3 types of equations/graphs	Partially correct display of 2 out of 3 types of equations/graphs	Visually appealing, correct display of all 3 types	Sophisticated display of all 3 types of graphs	
Written	• Evidence of reason • Supporting statistics	Unclear recommendation, no supporting data	Recommendation made without supporting data	Clear recommendation using supportive statistics	Insightful recommendation using supporting data	

Total Score _____

Scale	
A =	D =
B =	F =
C =	

Comments:

Figure 5.16

choose which pieces they believe represent their knowledge and understanding of key concepts. It is important however, that the items be graded according to *predetermined* criteria and indicators developed by the teacher and students.

Some teachers, however, choose another option. They do not tell the students which items they plan to grade until after the entire portfolio is submitted. These teachers want students to do quality work on *all* of the entries—not just the ones they know will be graded. Once the key items are selected, the teacher uses a rubric to grade the pieces fairly and consistently. (See Figure 5.17 for a sample rubric for a student dramatization.)

Each Entry Graded One-to-One (the Standards Portfolio)

Every item in the portfolio may be graded either before or after the final portfolio is submitted. The grades are determined by standards developed by the class and teacher or from scoring rubrics established by the school or district. The evaluation scale helps ensure consistency and fairness in the grading process. The advantage of this method is that students put a great deal of effort into all the entries because they know they will be evaluated. This type of portfolio often constitutes a large percentage of the total grade. Students usually know in advance what assignments will be graded and the criteria on which they will be evaluated. The disadvantage for teachers is the time involved in

Oral Presentation

Standard: The student gives an oral presentation.

Criteria	*Not Yet* 1	*In Progress* 2	*Meets Standard* 3	*Exceeds Standard* 4
Voice • Expression • Tone • Feeling	Used one element	Used two elements	Used three elements appropriately	Used all three elements effectively and enthusiastically
Volume	Could be heard by a few people in the room	Could be heard by people in front row only	Could be heard by most people in room	Could be heard clearly by all people in room
Enunciation	Could understand some words	Could understand most words	Could understand all of the words	Spoken like a professional actor
Content • Facts • Quotes • Statistics	• Used one element • Some inaccuracies	• Used two elements • Accurate information	• Used three elements • Accurate information • Current sources	• Used three elements • Accurate and current sources • Creative presentation

Figure 5.17

assessing portfolios when they are submitted, especially at the middle school and high school levels, where teachers can have as many as 150 students. Figure 5.18 is a sample evaluation of a videotaped speech from a portfolio. Another sample of a portfolio with individually graded items is provided in the Example 5.4 at the end of this chapter.

Sample Speech Rubric

Name of Speaker ___Eddie___

Title of Speech ___My summer in the country___

VOLUME

I couldn't hear you.	It was hard to hear you.	I heard you most of the time.	You were easy to hear.	SCORE
1	2	3	4	3

EYE CONTACT

You didn't use eye contact.	You hardly ever used eye contact.	Sometimes you made eye contact.	You had really good eye contact.	SCORE
1	2	3	4	2

VISUAL

Foul Ball (You had no visual or it wasn't right.)	A Walk (Your visual was good, but you didn't use it.)	R.B.I. (Your visual made your speech better.)	Grand Slam (Your visual was very creative.)	SCORE
1	2	3	4	4

FOCUS

Muddy (I wasn't sure what you meant.)	Foggy (Sometimes I didn't know what you meant.)	Fuzzy (Most of the time I knew what you meant.)	Crystal Clear (I always knew what you meant.)	SCORE
1	2	3	4	3

Comments: ___Eye contact would have made your speech a hit!___
___Creative use of visual aids—I loved the horse saddle! Great___
___speaking voice, too.___

> Scale
> 14–16 = A
> 10–13 = B
> 7–9 = C
> Below 6 = Not yet

Final Grade: ___B___

Figure 5.18

Before the enactment of NCLB federal legislation, several states were experimenting with portfolio assessment of state standards. Outside scorers assessed the portfolios using scoring rubrics that were developed by psychometricians and teachers to increase the reliability of the scoring process. These portfolios included entries that demonstrated that the student had met certain requirements. While most states must now use standardized tests for these purposes, several states continue to utilize the standards portfolio as alternative measures for students with special needs.

One Grade for Whole Portfolio—Blue Ribbon

Many teachers find that, regardless of whether individual items in the portfolio are graded, they grade the whole portfolio on the basis of specific generic criteria, such as creativity, completeness, organization, evidence of thoughtfulness, evidence of improvement, reflectivity, and quality of work. (See Blackline 5.6 at the end of this chapter.) Teachers assign a letter grade, point value, or percentage grade based on the organization of the entire portfolio. Grading the portfolio as a whole requires less time than grading each item individually, but it still provides specific feedback to the students (Figure 5.19).

Sample Criteria for Grading Portfolios

- Accuracy of information
- Completeness
- Connections to other subjects
- Creativity
- Development of process
- Diversity of selections
- Evidence of understanding
- Following directions

- Form (mechanics)
- Growth and development
- Insightfulness
- Knowledge of content
- Multiple intelligences
- Originality
- Persistence
- Quality product

- Reflectiveness
- Self-assessment
- Timeliness
- Transfer of ideas
- Variety of entries
- Visual appeal

Figure 5.19

Weighted Portfolio Rubric And Justice for All

Items in a graded final portfolio will often vary in their importance, and therefore should be weighed appropriately when determining the student's grade. Items can be weighed according to what the teacher and students are the most important elements, the major focus of learning, or the entries that showcase attainment of curriculum goals or standards. (Figure 5.20 presents sample weighted rubrics for specific assignments. For a weighted rubric for the entire portfolio, see Blackline 5.12 at the end of this chapter.)

Combination Portfolio—Potpourri

Teachers can also experiment with grading options or alternate them at different times of the year and for different purposes and types of portfolios.

Weighted Rubric for Portfolio

Student: _Debbie W._   Subject: _Language Arts_   Date: _Jan. 24_

Goal/Standard: Use reading, writing, listening, and speaking skills to research and apply information for specific purposes in a portfolio.

Criteria	Indicators	1	2	3	4	Score
Form	• Spelling • Grammar • Sentence structure	2–3 errors	1–2 errors	0 errors	0 errors and a high level of writing	$\underline{4} \times 3 = \underline{\frac{12}{(12)}}$
Visual Appeal	• Cover • Artwork • Graphics	Missing 2 elements	Missing 1 element	All 3 elements included	All 3 elements are creatively and visually appealing	$\underline{3} \times 4 = \underline{\frac{12}{(16)}}$
Organization	• Completeness • Time lines • Table of Contents	Missing 2 elements	Missing 1 element	All 3 elements included	All 3 elements demonstrate high level of organization	$\underline{4} \times 5 = \underline{\frac{20}{(20)}}$
Knowledge of Key Concepts	• Key concepts • Evidence of understanding • Application	No evidence of key concepts included in portfolio	Evidence of basic level of understanding of key concepts	Evidence of high level of understanding of key concepts	Evidence of ability to apply knowledge to new situations	$\underline{4} \times 6 = \underline{\frac{24}{(24)}}$
Reflections	• One per piece • Depth of reflection • Ability to self-assess	Missing 2 or more reflections	Missing 1 reflection	Insightful reflections for each piece	Reflections show insightfulness and ability to self-assess	$\underline{3} \times 7 = \underline{\frac{21}{(28)}}$

Scale

A = _93–100_
B = _87–92_
C = _78–86_
D = _below 78_

Final Score: _89/100_

Final Grade: _B_

Comments:

Nice job! Next time, be sure to pay more attention to visual appeal and reflection.

Figure 5.20

Standardized rubrics from school systems, districts, and states serve as models for preparation of guidelines to enable teachers to align classroom expectations and portfolio purposes with the standardized expectations and scoring instruments. Using global rubrics helps teachers to set expectations correlated to their students in the district or state, and not just at their own school.

GUIDELINES FOR GRADING PORTFOLIOS

Regardless of whether portfolios are graded or teachers or outside assessors evaluate the contents, portfolios present a portrait of a student as a learner who cannot be captured by checklists, anecdotal records, or report cards. According to Vavrus (1990), "the key to scoring a portfolio is in setting standards relative to your goals for student learning ahead of time. Portfolios can be evaluated in terms of standards of excellence or on growth demonstrated within a portfolio, rather than on comparisons made among different students' work" (p. 48). In other words, evaluation of portfolios is more similar to criterion-referenced tests than to norm-referenced tests.

One of the major purposes of portfolios is to trace a student's progress. The student may never pass the same test, meet the same standards, or earn an "A." However, the portfolio shows the student's entry level and the progress that he or she made. If a student started at Level 0 or "not yet" and progressed to Level 2, that student demonstrated growth toward meeting the goal or standard. The student, parent, and teacher should celebrate the journey and establish new goals to motivate the student to continue to improve. The guidelines in Figure 5.21 provide a framework for scoring portfolios. Teachers can adjust the guidelines to meet their purposes for scoring the portfolio. It is important, however, to share the scoring guidelines with the students before they complete their portfolio so that they know the expectations for completing quality work.

Guidelines for Scoring Portfolios

1. Make sure the portfolio is correlated with curriculum goals or standards.

2. Introduce the portfolio by telling students why they will be doing it and what the intended goal is (final grade, reflection, standards, integration).

3. Show examples of portfolios. (Try to show examples that are "not yet," some that are "OK" as well as some that are "awesome.")

4. Brainstorm a list of criteria that make up a portfolio (organization, reflection, connections, insights, goal setting).

5. Generate a list of indicators that specify the types of performances under each of the examples.

6. Create a scale that lists the indicators of each of the criteria on the scale (not yet, OK, awesome; below expectations, meets expectations, exceeds expectations; or 1, 2, 3, 4).

7. Give students some choice in their selection of items to include.

8. Have students prepare portfolios.

9. Share the portfolios with the class or outside audience (other classes, teachers, parents, exhibitions).

10. Ask peers to give feedback on portfolios.

11. Have the students self-evaluate by using a rubric to score their own portfolios.

12. Use the portfolio rubric to complete a teacher evaluation.

13. Discuss the portfolios with the students.

14. Provide feedback.

15. Determine a grade based on self-evaluations and teacher evaluations.

16. Have the student set new goals for his or her next portfolio.

Figure 5.21

Examples

●●●

My Self-Assessment: My Strengths and Problem Areas in Social Studies

Name: _____ Grade: _____ Date: _____

	Content/Subject Matter	I loved studying about Egypt, and I read three books on the pyramids. I feel like an expert.
My Strengths	Processes (writing, reading, thinking, etc.)	I really like to read. Some of the books I select are high school level, but I have no problems with them. I also like writing creative stories.
	Social Skills (cooperation, behavior)	I am a good organizer in the groups, and I always listen to others. Other group members respect my work.
	Content/Subject Matter	I receive low grades on research reports because I use only a few sources. I also tend to "copy" too much.
My Problem Areas	Processes (writing, reading, thinking, etc.)	I can't spell anything. I proofread, but I can't look up every single word. I'm a creative writer, but I can't stand using a dictionary or spell check.
	Social Skills (cooperation, behavior)	Sometimes I get impatient with my group. It takes too long for them to decide what to do! I'd rather do it myself sometimes because I can do a better job.

Example 5.1

My Learning Lists

Name ___Mindy___   Grade ___8th Mythology Unit___

Vocabulary terms and allusions I have learned:

He is an <u>Adonis.</u>	a <u>Herculean</u> task	a <u>hydra</u>-headed woman
a <u>titanic</u> problem	the <u>Midas</u> touch	<u>Medusa</u>-haired woman
<u>Pandora's</u> box	He worked like a <u>Trojan.</u>	<u>Cassandra</u> warning

---

Stories and books I have read:

"The Twelve Labors of Hercules"

The Iliad

The Odyssey

"Pandora's Box"

Stories and poems I have written:

"The First Super Bowl on Mt.Olympus"

"The Modern-Day Labors of Hercules"

"Original Myth to Explain How We Got Lightning Bugs"

Things I am having trouble with:

Working a video camera

Understanding Pythagorean Theorem

Working with a group

Important things I have learned:

How pride (hubris) and jealousy can be the downfall of all men and women

How many words come from Greek mythology

Example 5.2

Journal Stems for Student Reflection

Student: Penny

Date: Sept.10

Topic: Social Studies

Grade: 10

Select one of the following stem statements to use in your journal entry:

Stem Statements

A.   The best part about . . .

B.   An interesting part is . . .

C.   I predict . . .

D.   I wonder . . .

E.   How . . .

F.   Why . . .

G.   A connecting idea is . . .

H.   I believe . . .

Journal Entry:

I predict that P.E. classes will be required for all students through 12th grade. Right now it is an elective for 10th grade, but one of the most important things in life is staying healthy. Exercise is a life skill that is as important as English or math.

Example 5.3

Self-Assessment of an Oral Presentation

English Language Arts Standard 4.B:
Speak effectively using language appropriate to the situation and audience.

Middle/Junior High School Benchmark: 4.B.3a:
Deliver planned oral presentations using language and vocabulary appropriate to the purpose, message, audience; provide details and supporting information that clarify main ideas and use visual aids and contemporary technology as support.

Criteria/Performance Indicators:	Not Yet 0	Some Evidence ✓
Language and Vocabulary		
• Appropriate to the purpose		
• Appropriate to the message		
• Appropriate to the audience		
Information to Support and Clarify the Main Idea		
• Details		
• Examples		
• Statistics		
• Quotes		
• Anecdotes		
Visual Aids (select two)		
• Grapic organizer		
• Picture		
• Poster		
• Pamphlet		
• Costume		
Technology (select two)		
• Transparencies		
• Slides		
• PowerPoint		
• Videotape		
• Digital pictures		

Comments:

Scale
18–20 = A
16–17 = B
14–15 = C
Below 14 = Not Yet

Total Points: _____

Final Grade: _____

Example 5.4

T-chart Graphic Organizer

SKILL: Intelligent behavior; checking for accuracy

What does it look like?	What does it sound like?
Using spell check	"How do you spell *receive*?"
Using a dictionary	"Where is our grammar reference book?"
Checking sources	"Give me the thesaurus."
Having a peer read material	"Will you edit this for me?"
Proofreading carefully	"Let me check my figures again."
Reading aloud	"This is my third draft."
Using a calculator	

Self-assessment T-chart

Select one criterion or skill and complete a T-chart with your class.

Criterion/Skill: _____

What does it look like?	What does it sound like?

Example 5.5

Tools for Self-Assessment

Self-Assessment Checklist

☑ Self ☐ Peer ☐ Teacher

Student: _Ray_ Date: _April 11, 2001_

	Not Yet	Sometimes	Frequently
WORK HABITS:			
• Gets work done on time.	–	–	✓
• Asks for help when needed.	–	–	✓
• Takes initiative.	–	✓	–

Comments: *It's hard getting used to asking the group and teachers to help, but I'm getting better.*

	Not Yet	Sometimes	Frequently
STUDY SKILLS:			
• Organizes work.	–	–	✓
• Takes good notes.	–	✓	–
• Uses time well.	–	✓	–

Comments: *Since our base group has made this a goal, and we worked outside of class, I really am doing much better at this.*

	Not Yet	Sometimes	Frequently
SOCIAL SKILLS:			
• Works well with others.	–	–	✓
• Listens to others.	–	–	✓
• Helps others.	–	–	✓

Comments: *My group is great. We have really done good work on all our assignments. I've learned how to listen and help. My group has really helped me.*

Signed: _Ray_

Adapted from *How to Assess Authentic Learning* 3rd ed., by Kay Burke. © 1999 Corwin Press. Used with permission.

Double-Entry Journal

Student Name: _Ray_ Grade: _7_

Subject: _Social Studies_

Starting My Portfolio	Finishing My Portfolio
Oh no! Another notebook to keep. I always manage to lose it before the end of the quarter. This time we have to show it to other people besides the teacher. I don't know how to type, and I can't do artwork. I'm in big trouble!	I can't believe how hard I worked on this thing. I learned word processing because everyone else was typing theirs. I am pretty proud. Some of my friends read it and really liked it. My mom will love it. She'll probably show it to all the relatives.
I know I will have to become more organized or I'll fail!	I like the computer artwork I added. It makes my portfolio look professional.

Date: _9/1_ Date: _11/3_

Analysis of My Strengths and Challenges

Old Me (Challenges) | New Me (Strengths)

Old Me (Challenges):
- wrote one draft
- never proofread
- never showed work to others
- used verbal/linguistic intelligence
- never gave a thought to learning

New Me (Strengths):
- wrote 3 drafts
- used spell check
- had peers read everything
- used all eight intelligences
- reflected on my own thinking

I still need to improve in

| grammar |
| artwork |
| neatness |
| talking too much in groups |
| paraphrasing |

Signed: _Ray_

Goal Setting

Short-Term Goals (3 months)

1. Learn to use grammar check on computer.
2. Include 10 books in bibliography.
3. Learn to use the video camera.
4. Work on my interpersonal intelligence.

Long-Term Goals (6 months)

1. Learn to use computer graphics.
2. Take an art class as an elective.
3. Have someone in group tutor me in grammar.
4. Work on not interrupting others.

Ray's Goals

Target Date: _11/3_ (next portfolio conference)

Target Date: _5/8_ (final portfolio conference)

Comments: *I've decided I need to learn everything I can about technology (videos, computers) to succeed.*

Signed: _Ray_ Date: _11/5_

Example 5.6

Rubric for Assessing a Birthday Party

	1 *"I need to go home and do my homework!"*	2 *"Can't stay–I've got chores at home."*	3 *"Can I spend the night?"*	4 *"Will you adopt me?"*
Food	steamed broccoli and carrots	Mom's tuna fish and potato chip casserole	McDonald's Happy Meal (free balloons)	super deluxe pizza (deep dish)
Guitar Heroes	new underwear (Babys R Us specials)	school supplies (Mr. Eraserhead)	*Pirates of the Caribbean* video set	Hannah Montana CD
Entertainment	my sister's poetry readings (T.S. Eliot)	polka music (accordion rap song)	*Dora the Explorer and Friends*	*High School Musical*
Games	"Go Fish!" and "Slap Jack"	musical chairs to Broadway show tunes	virtual reality headsets	full contact Twister (no chaperones)

Example 5.7

Student Peer Assessment

On a scale from 1 to 5, rate your group on the following items.

All members contributed equally to the project.	1	2	3	**4**	5
Our group worked well together.	1	2	3	**4**	5
Disagreed with the idea, not the person.	1	2	3	**4**	5
Stayed on task and helped others do the same.	1	2	3	**4**	5
Encouraged group members.	1	2	3	4	**5**
I would like to work with these students again.	1	2	3	4	**5**

1 = Strongly Disagree   **2** = Disagree   **3** = Agree   **4** = Strongly Agree   **5** = Couldn't agree more!

Comments: My group made me *want* to do my best on this assignment. We got along well and completed the project on time. Cooperative learning is great!

Student Name: Leticia

Example 5.8

Primary/Special Needs Student Selection Tools

I Can Do It!

This is my goal for next month!

I need to get better at listening for directions. I want to get better at math problems too.

Student Signature

Tyler

This is my teacher's goal for me!

I agree with your goals, Tyler. I think that you will be able to meet your goals. I will help you.

Teacher Signature

Ms.Smithson

This is my parents' goal for me!

I can see that you have met with your teacher about your problem listening. I know you are smart and will do better when you improve. Dad and I will help you too.

Parent's Signature

Mom

Example 5.9

My Best Work in Science

Name: Pranjali A

Date: December 1, 2006

This is an example of my best work in science.

When I used to think about science, I got tired. Now, I feel great because I can do the experiments and write up good lab reports.

Example 5.10

Portfolio Rubric

Name: <u>Seung L</u>   Subject: <u>Science</u>   Grade: <u>5</u>

Directions: Develop criteria and indicators for assessing the final portfolio.

Criteria	Does Not Meet Expectations 1	In Progress 2	Meets Expectations 3	Exceeds Expectations 4
Online Lab				
1. Pretest		2		
2. Processes			3	
3. Quiz				4
Application				
1. Plan			3	
2. Construction			3	
3. Write-Up				4
Project				
1. Technology				4
2. Information			3	
3. Completeness				4
Final				
1. Lab				4
2. Test				4
3. Write-Up				4

Comments:
I chose this work because I did not know anything about wind before this unit. Now I even know a lot about wind turbines.

Scale
A = 44–48
B = 38–43
C = 32–37
D = 28–32

Final Score: <u>42</u>

Final Grade: <u>B</u>

Example 5.11

Blacklines

My Learning Lists

Name: _____   Class: _____   Date: _____

Vocabulary terms I have learned:

Things I have read:

Things I have written:

Things I am having trouble with:

Important things I have learned:

Blackline 5.1

Pictorial Reflective Rubric

Pictorial Checklist

How did you feel about this activity?

How did you feel about this activity?

How did you feel about this activity?

Would you like to do this activity again?

Comments:

Blackline 5.2

Self-Assessment T-chart

Select one criterion or skill and complete a T-chart with your class.

Criterion/Skill: _____

What does it look like?	*What does it sound like?*

Blackline 5.3

Self-Assessment Checklist

Criteria	Not Yet	Almost There	Got It
Indicators: 1.			
2.			
3.			
4.			
5.			
6.			
7.			

Blackline 5.4

Scoring Rubric

Select an item in the portfolio and create a rubric to grade it.

Standard: _____

Assignment: _____

CRITERIA	INDICATORS	1	2	3	4	
1.						**SCORE** ___ x 5 ___ (20)
2.						___ x 5 ___ (20)
3.						___ x 5 ___ (20)
4.						___ x 5 ___ (20)
5.						___ x 5 ___ (20)

Comments:

SCALE

A =
B =
C =
D =

Final Score: _____ (100)

Final Grade: _____

Blackline 5.5

Portfolio Rubric

Name: _____   Subject: _____   Grade: _____

Directions: Develop criteria and indicators for assessing the final portfolio.

Criteria	Does Not Meet Expectations 1	In Progress 2	Exceeds Expectations 3	Expectations 4
[ ]				
1.				
2.				
3.				
[ ]				
1.				
2.				
3.				
[ ]				
1.				
2.				
3.				
[ ]				
1.				
2.				
3.				

Comments:

Scale
A = _____
B = _____
C = _____
D = _____

Final Score: _____

Final Grade: _____

Blackline 5.6

Peer Review of a Portfolio

Student Name: _____ Date: _____

Subject: _____

Strengths of this piece of work:

_____

_____

_____

Weaknesses of this piece of work:

_____

_____

_____

_____

How the captions could be improved:

_____

_____

_____

On the rubric I would rate it as _____

What I would have to do to turn this into a/an ____ -grade project:

_____

_____

_____

Some other suggestions I have for you:

_____

_____

_____

What it helps me think of for adding or changing my own project:

_____

_____

_____

Blackline 5.7

"Rate Your Mate" Secondary Peer Assessment

Please use the following criteria to assess your partner/team member's contribution to the task.

Evaluating My Partner/Team Member	1	2	3
Motivation			
Work			
Contribution			
Comments:			

Blackline 5.8

Double-Entry Journal

Student: _____   Grade: _____

Subject: _____

Date: _____   Date: _____

Starting My Portfolio	*Upon Completion of My Portfolio*

Signed: _____   Signed: _____

Blackline 5.9

Parent Portfolio Artifact Selection

Date: _____

To: Parent/Significant Other

Please review the attached entries that may be included in _____ 's
portfolio and provide your feedback.   (student's name)

Which piece most surprises you? Why?

Which piece do you feel needs more work? Why?

Which piece do you want to include in the portfolio? Why?

Signature: _____

Date: _____

Blackline 5.10

Final Portfolio

Student: _____ Grade: _____ Date: _____

Selection	Teacher Comments
1.	
2.	
3.	
4.	
5.	

Blackline 5.11

Weighted Rubric for Portfolio

Student: _____   Subject: _____   Date: _____

Goal/Standard: _____

_____

Criteria	Indicators	1	2	3	4	Score
Forma	• Spelling • Grammar • Sentence structure	2–3 errors	1–2 errors	0 errors	0 errors and a high level of writing	__ x 3 =___ (12)
Visual Appeal	• Cover • Artwork • Graphics	Missing 2 elements	Missing 1 element	All 3 elements included	All 3 elements are creatively and visually appealing	__ x 4 = ___ (16)
Organization	• Completeness • Timeliness • Table of Contents	Missing 2 elements	Missing 1 element	All 3 elements included	All 3 elemeants demonstrate high level of organization	__ x 5 = ___ (20)
Knowledge of Key Concepts	• Key concepts • Evidence of understanding • Application	Little evidence of key concepts included in portfolio	Evidence of basic level of understanding of key concepts	Evidence of high level of understanding of key concepts	Evidence of ability to apply knowledge to new situations	__ x 6 = ___ (24)
Reflections	• One per piece • Depth of reflection • Ability to self-assess	Missing 2 or more reflections	Missing 1 reflection	Insightful reflections for each piece	Reflections show insightfulness and ability to self-assess	__ x 7 = ___ (28)

Comments:

Scale

A = _____
B = _____
C = _____
D = _____

Final Score: _____
(100)

Final Grade: _____

Blackline 5.12

6

Connect Students' Voices Through Web Conferences and Showcases

OVERVIEW

Through regular and ongoing reflection and self-evaluation, students come to value their work as representing who they are and what they can do. Even though students may have done their very best work up to this point, the conclusion of the portfolio process requires them to prepare for the essence of portfolios—the communication and acknowledgment of who they are as learners. At the last stage of the portfolio development process, students are given the opportunity to showcase or give voice to their achievements and successes as learners. They are given the opportunity to show how they have met or exceeded standards or how they have achieved the purposes of the portfolio. Artifacts showing "clear and compelling" evidence of achievement are enhanced when students take one more reflective stance and reveal their perceptions and attitudes about the effort expended and the outcomes derived from learning. Parents, teachers, and the public in general are invited to view evidence in the portfolio or e-portfolio that tells the story of how and why students have met portfolio purposes, curriculum goals, or standards.

This chapter describes how the preparation for and engagement in a portfolio conference or online showcase helps teachers, parents, and students recognize the outcomes of the academic content and context of the learning experience. The conversations related to students' evidence of accomplishment provide valuable insights into their understanding. This significant stage of the portfolio process will be covered in this chapter.

The final stage of the portfolio or e-portfolio will ideally result in students and teachers recognizing together the significance of each student's unique learning achievement. At the conclusion of this stage, students are ready to invite observations and discussions about their work, their goals, and even alternative strategies that may be used to meet future academic goals. Portfolio exhibitions and showcases that culminate the portfolio process celebrate student learning and achievement by allowing parents, guardians, and others to view and respond to the story of each student's learning. The procedures, tools, and reflections that comprise this important part of portfolios will be provided throughout this chapter.

INTRODUCTION

While the most common purpose of using academic portfolios is to promote and show evidence of student achievement, it is increasingly recognized that portfolios in schools today enhance the assessment of the learning process. By including the actual artifacts that show evidence of students' development and achievement of learning standards, portfolios extend and deepen the assessment process beyond test scores or grade point averages. The value and multiple uses for student portfolios have become apparent at all grade levels as they are used in more and more schools.

With the accomplishment of print and e-portfolios, students, teachers, and parents recognize the communication impact that they provide. While top-performing students often have their portfolios announced to their communities, *all* students want an opportunity to show their academic achievement to the world beyond the classroom. As the potential of portfolios' value is recognized, teachers and administrators who promote them will find that their students' accomplishments are better communicated to interested audiences and stakeholders in their schools' communities—thus promoting student motivation.

In addition to being a significant educational event, the portfolio conference, or Web showcase, has evolved into an artistic and technological opportunity for students. With careful, thoughtful preparation, they can skillfully present students' academic achievement and communicate their learning dispositions and talents to others. The portfolio conference, exhibition, or Web showcase brings each student's work and accomplishments alive. As students present the content of their portfolio or e-portfolio to others, they celebrate and enjoy their accomplishments while the viewers gain valuable insight into students' "heads" about their knowledge and understanding of key curricular objectives.

As teachers guide their students in the conclusion of the portfolio process, the role of student reflection and inquiry becomes apparent. Reflective inquiry occurs through conversations with teachers, peers, and others, helping students to see their learning experiences in different ways. In the ongoing critiques and conversations about their portfolios, students demonstrate their abilities as truly reflective learners, who always act with intention (Harste et al.,

1984). The very act of explaining their learning evidence helps students rehearse and reinforce their understanding at even deeper levels. Through portfolio conferences, exhibitions, and Web showcases, students' previous engagement in acquiring self-knowledge and capacities for self-reflection on the learning processes culminates in the true essence of portfolios: to value (Barrett, 2006). (See Example 6.1 at the end of this chapter.)

Portfolio conferences, exhibitions, and Web showcases have become viable tools for promoting sustained student motivation and gaining new understanding of students' accomplishments and connections to learning and development. Benson and Barnett (2005) note that the conference performance is the assessment performance that truly demonstrates student learning (p. viii). During the preparations for the final portfolio conference or Web showcase, students can conference with their teachers and trade places with their peers. As they do, they participate even more reflectively in the process of valuing and respecting other students' academic work and progress. Fellow students not only view peer work but also scrutinize the work and offer informed critiques using familiar assessments.

Preparation for the Portfolio Conferences and Online Web Showcase

Following weeks or months of student engagement in reflection, self-assessment, and practice with both creating and using scoring rubrics and checklists, students are almost ready for the most exciting stage of the portfolio process—the portfolio conference or online Web showcase. It is at this time when each piece included in the portfolio will be reexamined by the student. It will require several "metacognitive moments" when students will plan, monitor, and evaluate the value of the artifact, both as an individual piece and in relation to the whole portfolio (Figure 6.1).

It is in this explicit reflection that students address the "learn to learn" skills embedded in the standards of learning. Rolheiser and colleagues (2000) define reflection as "ideas or conclusions that are a result of your thinking about your work. These ideas are connected to specific criteria and may help you determine future goals and actions" (p. 40). Among the "learn to learn"

Reflective Tools

- Planning
- Goal setting
- Self-assessment
- Self-monitoring
- Self-regulation
- Self-evaluation

Figure 6.1

standards (Figure 6.2) are skills needed for problem solving and decision making in real-world situations. These reflective tools include planning, goal setting, self-assessment, self-monitoring, self-regulation, and self-evaluation. This particular process standard falls into a category of cognitive skills often referred to as metacognition.

"Learn to Learn" Standards

Students demonstrate within and integrate across all content areas the ability to

1. Develop, monitor, and revise plans of action to meet deadlines and accomplish goals;

2. Identify problems and define their scope and elements;

3. Review and revise communications to improve accuracy;

4. Apply acquired information, ideas, and skills to different contexts; and

5. Develop and apply strategies based on one's own experience in preventing and solving problems.

Figure 6.2

From *Show-Me Standards.* © 1993 by the Missouri Department of Elementary and Secondary Education.

At the final stage of the portfolio process, teachers can have students determine what the final portfolio will look like by "running through their minds" to recall significant academic achievements. Students might try to visualize their actual portfolio exhibition or Web showcase and how they will receive favorable comments from their viewers. They then return to the contents of their portfolios, noting the items that are accompanied by the written reflections that were placed in the portfolio at the time the piece was first included. Next, they make decisions to keep items or revise their earlier visions of achieving portfolio goals. Here students might develop strategies for future success. For example, one student reflection taped to a drawing was, "Before I did this project, I envisioned what my invention would look like. This is the first sketch I made." At the conclusion of the portfolio review, the student will probably write, "Now I am amazed at how my original idea ended up with what I actually created!"

This example demonstrates how easy it is for students to look back on earlier work and then create new reflections as final portfolio pieces are selected. By using a tag or label for each piece, the student explains the value of the artifact and its significance to the purpose of the academic portfolio. Each of these tags, labels, reflective comments, and ideas inserted by the student provides a running monologue. This monologue will bring the portfolio alive for the viewer who has not yet taken part in the development of the portfolio, or who has not had an opportunity to discuss the portfolio with its creator. Stems that promote student reflections on items in the portfolio are displayed in Blackline 6.6 at the end of this chapter.

As has been shown in previous chapters, the portfolio and e-portfolio offer in distinct ways robust opportunities for ongoing metacognitive reflection. As students first develop their portfolios, they survey the overall scheme for their portfolio and *plan* what their goals are. Then, they may shift automatically into a *monitoring* mode when each additional artifact is weighed against the whole portfolio. And, of course, students naturally *evaluate* as they reflect on why the piece is valued and the reason it should be included in the finished portfolio (Burke, 2005). As students begin to prepare for their portfolio conferences or Web showcases, the accomplishments that occurred at the initial and beginning stages—including goal setting about their learning—are revisited. They are well prepared to celebrate and enjoy their accomplishments, while the viewers will gain valuable insight into the students' knowledge and understanding of key curricular objectives—as well as insight into their gifts and talents. (See Blackline 6.7 at the end of this chapter.)

In each of the following types of portfolio conferences, showcases, or exhibitions an effective plan will consist of several steps. First, teachers need to consider the conference purposes that best align with their students' needs, learning dispositions, and goals. Next, they need to make decisions about who the audience will be and when the conferences will take place. Once this is determined, they are ready to engage students in the remainder of the conference planning process. Some considerations necessary to prepare for the presentation of portfolios or e-portfolios are the allotted time frame, media (technology) options, personal style, and other concerns (Figure 6.3). At this point, the "how" of the conference can be mapped out with students.

Teacher-Student Portfolio Conferences

When preparing students for final portfolio conferences and exhibitions, teachers recognize that critics will come to the showing, and "the rubber will meet the road." Teachers who value students' dialogue about learning and achievement schedule regular individual conferences during the portfolio process, where students select artifacts, and describe and reflect on their significance. Here, at the final stage of portfolio collection, selection, and reflection, teachers once again "sit beside" the student to value what has been accomplished and how the pieces show evidence of achievement. These conferences help students in reviewing their accomplishments and "recognizing how successful they were, and facilitating new experiences where they can apply their learning" (Silvers, 1994, p. 27).

At a time when national legislation for schools requires schools to provide compelling evidence of student achievement through standardized tests, teacher-student portfolio conferences can become a meaningful and authentic process that helps both teachers and students recognize the depth and dimensionality of the knowledge and skills demonstrated through evidence. For these conferences, students either reflect on pieces that teachers have already selected, or select and reflect on portfolio entries on their own. Here they will identify

---

What Will Be the Goals of the Portfolio or E-portfolio Conference?

Is the presentation for a peer conference or a student-led parent conference?

Is the presentation going to be digital or online?

Is the presentation for a class exhibition or a schoolwide portfolio showcase?

What reflections do learners need to engage in?

Will students need to compare their achievement to benchmarks and learning standards?

Will the portfolio need to show progress over time?

Will it show achievement of individual learning goals and achievements?

What questions should the students prepare for their audience?

Who is the audience?

    What are they looking for?

    How are they going to view the work?

    Are they familiar with the type of work?

    What can be done to maximize interest and understanding?

How do they wish to evaluate the conferences?

Is there a particular format and scoring rubric to follow?

Will they evaluate the contents and the reflections?

Will they focus on social skills and communication?

Will they evaluate the audience's reaction to what they learned about the students as readers, writers, thinkers, problem solvers, etc.?

Figure 6.3

artifacts that they believe demonstrate the accomplishment of content standards, the quality of academic products and performances, and the significance of subject area learning. These portfolio conferences connect the parallel processes of standards-based instruction with students' authentic learning.

Peer Portfolio or E-portfolio Conferences

It is a natural step for teachers to plan a peer portfolio or e-portfolio conference at the conclusion of the portfolio process. These ongoing student-led conferences promote student monitoring of progress toward individual goals, while they develop their social skills. Peer conferences are another opportunity to promote student voice in reviewing the goals of their portfolios and determining how best to present the portfolio at future student-led conferences, exhibitions, or Web showcases. Student peers help one another to select, reflect on, and write about those pieces that will best succeed in making their creators' work and achievement come alive. They help one another focus learning back onto the individual student who really knows best what has been learned.

During preparations for and participation in the peer portfolio conference, students will need to monitor how they have integrated the criteria for a finished portfolio (Figure 6.4). It is important for students to identify how thoughtfulness, deep understanding of subject matter, and growth in knowledge and skills are reflected in one another's portfolios. Similarly, they help one another compare and analyze each portfolio to ensure that there are both presence and diversity of entries that show accomplishment of portfolio purposes or performance standards. (See Example 6.5 and Blackline 6.4 at the end of this chapter.)

Criteria for a Finished Portfolio

Criteria for a finished portfolio might include several of the following:

Thoughtfulness (including evidence of students' monitoring of their own comprehension, metacognitive reflection, and productive habits of mind)

Growth and development in relationship to key curriculum expectancies and indicators

Understanding and application of key processes

Completeness, correctness, and appropriateness of products and processes presented in the portfolio

Diversity of entries (e.g., use of multiple formats to demonstrate achievement of designated performance standards)

Figure 6.4

Students often become highly motivated, excited, and a bit nervous when they know that the time has come to reveal their past and present accomplishments, knowledge, and talents. Like the artist preparing for an exhibition, they are eager to use relevant criteria that meet known standards or expectations. They want to be clear and coherent in describing the knowledge, skills, and dispositions they had to acquire and apply as they achieved the outcomes of difficult or time-intensive projects and performances. And, like the artist, they want to be sure that they show the diversity or range of the accomplishments. They hope to be articulate in expressing their pride of accomplishment or the reasons that they value or need a piece to "speak" for them. This is why the peer portfolio conference that occurs within the safety of the classroom community is so important to the success of exhibits of students' academic portfolios.

A successful strategy to promote engaging and meaningful peer portfolio conferences is the "Two-Four-Eight" conference. Students begin with a partner with whom they are comfortable and with whom they share all of their portfolio artifacts. Peers ask questions (Figure 6.5) that help the students to think more about each piece and to describe its significance in depth. The partners assist one another in selecting one or two artifacts that they will share in the next "round" of the conference. When the partners have completed their sharing, they find another partner. Now Partners A introduce the portfolio items that were selected by Partners B. When all have shown and given feedback to the selected items, each student selects a "favorite" or "best" artifact from the portfolio. Now the quads form a group of eight. Each person in the group of eight has one minute to talk about the selected final item. Following the close of the sharing, teachers may ask students to complete a conference evaluation form (Portfolio Reflection Questions for Partners) that helps them reflect on the contents of their portfolios as well as how they felt about their communication during the Two-Four-Eight. (See Example 6.4 and Blackline 6.2 at the end of this chapter.)

One secondary school teacher found that students were so anxious about being conversant enough in their portfolio conferences that she first had them face the wall to discuss their portfolios. While this might sound unusual, it is actually common for students to believe they need to "rehearse" the conversation they wish to have about something as personal as their creative or academic work.

Student-Led Portfolio Conference With Parents and Significant Others

In the student-led portfolio conference, students have the opportunity to communicate the evidence of their achievement to their parents or significant others (with teacher input and facilitation when needed). The response and

---

Peer Portfolio Conferences

Directions for the "Two-Four-Eight" Portfolio Showcase

1. Find a partner with whom you feel comfortable sharing all the items in your portfolio. Use the Portfolio Reflection Questions for Partners as a guide.

2. When you and your partner have completed your sharing of each portfolio, complete the Portfolio Reflection Questions for Partners. Then locate another pair to form a "quad." It is your responsibility to introduce your partner's portfolio and to describe the items that show the evidence of meeting portfolio purposes. Your partner then responds to comments, questions, or suggestions that the group offers. Each person then selects his or her strongest or most satisfying artifact to bring to the next round of sharing.

3. As each "quad" completes the steps in Item 2, its members must locate another quad that is ready to move to Step 3. It is here that each person shares his or her portfolio and showcases the single item that has been selected. The members of the group offer comments and suggestions as each person presents.

Figure 6.5

NOTE: Upon completion of the sharing, each participant will complete the Portfolio Conference Evaluation.

comments they receive in the dialogue with their parents promote real satisfaction and pride in each student. "Evaluation continues the spirit of inquiry by providing one more chance to ask questions—and one more opportunity to learn. Evaluation occurs as learners take reflective stances in relation to their work and then invite others in to have conversations about it" (Crafton & Burke, 1994, p. 5). Student-led conferences represent a highly effective way to communicate directly and authentically with parents. When students are directors of the reporting process, information can be communicated in a form everyone can understand and use. The portfolio and e-portfolio allow the student to become a significant part of the parent-teacher conference. Reviewing the pieces that will be placed in the final portfolio with parents both before and during the conference becomes a learning experience not only for the student but also for everyone involved. Parents who might not ordinarily feel involved and knowledgeable about the curricular expectations and performances of their student develop more familiarity and ease. Thus, student-led conferences are an especially important part of the comprehensive reporting system (Guskey & Bailey, 2001, pp. 190–191). (See Example 6.11 at the end of this chapter.)

When the student enters and leads the dialogue, the parent-teacher conference becomes more learner-centered. In effect, it has become a student-led parent conference. When the student plans, conducts, and evaluates the presentation of portfolio entries to be shared with parents (or significant others), the teacher takes a secondary role. In reality, the teacher facilitates the dialogue between parent and student at key places but encourages the student to assume responsibility for the conference's success. The students are ultimately responsible for their own learning and should not have to rely on the teacher alone to talk "about" their learning. Benson and Barnett (2005) believe there are many benefits of student-led conferences with parents. These benefits are shown in Figure 6.6.

If twenty-first-century schools are to move toward more learner-centered curricula and inquiry-based learning, one of the greatest challenges will be informing parents of these practices and explaining the professional and scientific knowledge base that supports them. Portfolio conferences address the concerns of parents by demonstrating their child's overall learning and achievement in the context of the instructional methodologies.

Benefits of Student-Led Conferencing

- Involve more parents
- Increase student motivation
- Meet state standards
- Improve student and teacher accountability
- Celebrate learning
- Make teaching more satisfying

Figure 6.6

Student-led portfolio conferences enable parents to learn about standards and curricular goals as they view and hear about their child's real learning experiences. (See Example 6.9 at the end of this chapter.) They see evidence of authentic learning that includes products from hands-on activities, increasingly difficult problem-solving activities, and successful teamwork. While interviewing their children as they display artifacts of learning from their portfolios, parents have the opportunity to see the connection between the active learning process and learning itself. Parents become less cautious, more trusting, and more enthusiastic about the transformation from a traditional teacher conference to the student-led conference. Students who are given the opportunity to lead the examination of their portfolios become convincing ambassadors of a school's success in meeting rigorous learning standards at all levels. Stiggins (2002), an authority on authentic learning and assessment, believes the student-led portfolio conference is "the biggest breakthrough to happen in communicating about student achievement in the past century" (p. 500).

The Portfolio Exhibition

When the portfolio conference is opened up to a schoolwide or community-based event, it is referred to as an *exhibition* or *showcase*. This type of portfolio conference is instrumental in promoting important connections among students and parents, family and community members, and concerned local businesspeople. Communitywide exhibitions and showcases offer the potential to reestablish the critical links between schools and families and between schools and communities.

As teachers and students become more confident with portfolio assessments and conferences, schoolwide exhibitions may become as commonplace as science fairs. The type of portfolio exhibited at these events may vary, but it is often the portfolio of significant achievement (best work) or the standards portfolio. Most typically, the purpose of the exhibition is to showcase the quality as well as the individual learning characteristics of the students. Hence, the portfolio for the exhibition is often referred to as the showcase portfolio.

One of the reasons to offer the more public exhibition of the portfolio is to increase either schoolwide or public awareness of the performance and achievement occurring within the school. Some other reasons are shown in Figure 6.7.

The E-portfolio Web Showcase

When the portfolio to be exhibited is in a digital form, it makes sense that it be presented as an e-portfolio. This is a digital container that stores visual and auditory content. Because of its multimedia nature, it is produced with a wide variety of software tools. The e-portfolio becomes a container that seamlessly holds a variety of student work, together with the original assessments. When organized correctly, the e-portfolio leads its viewer to a satisfying and engaging review of the evidence the student presents. The e-portfolio can easily reveal unique aspects of its creator's learning process. It is easily shared among students in peer conferences as they either look on a computer together or participate in a class. Alternatively, it is viewed in a Web showcase where students display their e-portfolios using a classroom monitor or LCD projector. We like to distinguish

> # Reasons for a Portfolio Exhibition
>
> **Choose Conference Goals**
>
> **PORTFOLIO CONFERENCE GOALS SET BY STUDENTS**
>
> **Primary**
>
> *I want my portfolio to tell my story about how I learned to read this year.*
>
> **Intermediate**
>
> *By the time my parents are done looking at my portfolio and talking to me about my work and the reflections I have written, I want them to beas excited as I am about how much I have improved in everything!*
>
> **High School**
>
> *My portfolio conference should show the teachers in this school that I have really learned how to use computers to organize and present a project on communications.*

Figure 6.7

between a portfolio exhibition as described previously and an e-portfolio Web showcase, reserving the term *showcase* for the media presentation that the Internet provides. Schools have moved toward the use of technology and communication tools, making it is possible to hold Web-based e-portfolio showcases of student work and achievement. (See Example 6.3 at the end of this chapter.)

Technology helps student work come to life in the Web showcase because visual and auditory files are easily uploaded and linked to the e-portfolio. Students have many options when preparing for a Web showcase. They can use Web page–editing software to organize and present artifacts of all varieties, they can attach written tags and labels to each artifact, or they can record vocal reflections on the selected items.

PLANNING THE CONFERENCE, EXHIBITION, AND SHOWCASE

When planning for portfolio conferences, exhibitions, and showcases, teachers first need to consider the purposes that best meet their students' needs and learning dispositions. Next, they make decisions about who the audience will be and when the presentation will take place.

Mapping out the plan

Once this is determined, teachers are ready to engage students in the conference-planning process. Some considerations necessary for preparing for the presentation of portfolios are the allotted time frame, media (technology) options, personal style, and other concerns. At this point, the "how" of the conference can be mapped out with students. (See Blackline 6.9 at the end of this chapter.)

Part of mapping out the "how" of the conference is considering the logistics. Dates need to be scheduled, and setup needs to be arranged. The time frame should also be determined. Will there be time for the entire process, or will there be just a "Ready? Set! GO!" approach? What technology or media will be used? Is there a class video segment or audiotape that needs to be included? If media are part of the class or schoolwide presentation, how are they to be incorporated into the overall plan?

Strategies for introducing the portfolio or inviting questions from the audience need to be carefully considered with the students so the students can be prepared ahead of time. Here, the personal style of each student presenter needs to be considered. While engaged in their peer portfolio conferences, students were encouraged to use the opportunity to practice the art of anticipating the types of questions that would be asked about their portfolio entries and formulating appropriate responses. Now they are preparing for their conferences with parents and significant others. This is especially important when students are using e-portfolios for publishing on a Web site because they are not face-to-face with their audience.

Most students at all grade levels respond positively to brainstorming the possibilities for sharing academic portfolios with others. For example, students will select an appropriate type of presentation, rehearse as needed in front of a mirror or wall, and practice with a trusted friend or relative. The same ongoing teacher guidance that earlier supported the self-reflection process now prepares students for portfolio conferences, exhibitions, and Web showcases. Students can be guided in determining how to present each artifact or the overall content of their portfolios to their audiences in the most engaging and informative manner. Through the conversations that occur at portfolio conferences, exhibitions, and showcases, students demonstrate more ease and ability in becoming reflective and independent learners. Each student achieves voice as a person "who self-initiates, problem solves, reflectively evaluates learning, collaborates, and shows concern for, and engages in complex thinking strategies" (Crafton, 1991, p. 94). (See Blackline 6.10 at the end of this chapter.)

Conference Planning

- Consider purpose of portfolio and conference/exhibition
- Decide who the audience will be
- Choose when
- Map out what and how
- Schedule dates and times
- Plan setup

FOCUSING THE CONFERENCE

Significant Achievement—It Counts!

Portfolio and e-portfolio conferences give students the opportunity to present evidence of their significant achievements and talents across selected areas of the curriculum. For these conferences, they might include pieces that promote reflection on teacher-graded work, selected learning logs, projects or performances that demonstrate abilities and talents, or significant improvements on standardized test scores.

Goal Setting—Goal Post

The focus for goal-setting conferences is on students' previously set goals and includes reflections and self-assessments of how they have reached their goals. Portfolios would include pieces that highlight how students have matched, met, or surpassed their goals. In some instances, a student will need to select a "not yet" piece and discuss the strategies that he or she will employ to achieve the goal in the future. (See Example 6.6 at the end of this chapter.)

Single Learning Process Areas—Invitational

Students compile portfolio artifacts that reflect each indicator of a certain process, such as becoming an effective writer, for these learning process conferences. They use the standards and criteria originally applied to scoring and reflect on how they have developed in these areas. Students can include several artifacts to represent different audiences and invite responses through conference guides created ahead of time. (See Blackline 6.3 at the end of this chapter.)

Personally Satisfying Pieces—I Like It!

When student development has been the guiding purpose of the portfolio or e-portfolio, students will be encouraged to select pieces that are most satisfying to them as learners. They will use this conference to display how they have grown over time as readers, writers, group members, intelligent thinkers, or overall students. While the portfolio pieces shared in the conferences may represent many or a few of the subject areas or learning processes, they will represent achievements about which the students (their parents or teachers) feel best.

Joint Work—Join In

These portfolio conferences are often used in exhibitions and Web showcases to meet the group, class, or schoolwide purposes. Students present how they have succeeded as communities of learners in a variety of cooperative or collaborative projects and experiences.

Overall Portfolio—The Big Picture

This is, perhaps, the most important conference of all because it requires students to reflect on and self-assess strengths, weaknesses, successes, and failures across the curriculum. This conference represents the holistic picture of their performances and dispositions toward learning. In the conference, students call attention to those pieces that best represent who they are as learners throughout all the selected areas. A student may write (or audio record for a voice-over in an e-portfolio showcase) a reflective summary for each selection or create an audience guide (see Figure 6.7) that explains his or her characteristics as a learner. The "big picture" conference encourages students to value and celebrate the many ways in which they are developing as learners.

The Web Showcase

The e-portfolio not only excels in its application of maintaining student portfolios over time but is also an exciting platform on which students can showcase their talents, achievements, and evidence of meeting standards. The e-portfolio promotes a seamless review by audiences as its technology moves the reader from one part of the portfolio to another. Excitement is promoted by the integration of "hypermedia" presentations of slides, animation, audio voice-overs, or video clips. The planning process for a Web-based portfolio presentation parallels each of the portfolio processes described earlier. The planning process of the Web showcase also resembles the teacher's consideration of the "logistics" for the paper portfolio conference or exhibition and includes additional decision making regarding Web site publishing and monitoring for the safety and security of the students. This requires that school or district information technology staff be included in the decisions regarding student e-portfolios published on the Internet.

WHO IS INVOLVED, AND WHEN DO THEY CONFERENCE?

After choosing the purpose and focus of the portfolio conference, the teacher and students can decide *who* will participate in the conference and *when*. As discussed earlier, portfolio conferences or e-portfolio showcases blend seamlessly with traditional parent conferences or end-of-the-grading periods in curriculum and instruction. Depending on the purpose, teachers may select the *who* and *when* of portfolio conferences from a full palette of choices (Figure 6.8).

Choose Conference Goals—Scoring the Goal

Getting the portfolio ready is only one part of the story. Planning an effective presentation means that the goal must be clearly defined. Is the primary goal one of self-evaluation and self-reflection through the sharing with peers or parents? Is the primary goal a summative evaluation by the teacher? Is the goal to inform and impress a third party about the talent of the person presenting the portfolio? Whatever the goal may be, students need to zero in on it. The student may use this formula to set his or her goal:

1. Write the goal in a journal or notebook to clarify it in your mind.

2. Dialogue with a partner to articulate the goal in your own words.

3. Discuss the goal with a teacher or a parent.

4. Visualize the presentation and see yourself achieving the goal.

Possibilities for the Who and When of Portfolio Conferences

Connections to Authentic Learner Involvement—Connecting

Student-Student	Monthly
Pen Pal/Tech Pal	Quarterly
Multiage Students	By Semester
Student-Parent-Teacher	Quarterly
Portfolio Exhibition/Showcase—Everyone	Year-End

Teacher Accountability—Accounting for Learning Standards

Student-Teacher	Monthly
Student-Parent-Teacher	Quarterly
Student-Parent	By Semester
Portfolio Exhibition/Showcase—Everyone	Year-End

Parental Satisfaction with Learner Performance—Pleasing

Student-Teacher	Monthly
Student-Student	Quarterly
Student-Parent Home Conferences	By Semester
Student-Parent-Teacher	Quarterly
Portfolio Exhibition/Showcase—Everyone	Year-End

Outside Evaluations of the Success of Teaching and Learning—Evaluating

Student-Student (Cooperative Group Members)	Monthly
Multiage Student	Bimonthly
Student-Parent Home Conferences	By Semester
Significant Other	Quarterly
Pen Pal/Tech Pal	Quarterly
Schoolwide/Communitywide Portfolio Exhibitions/Showcase—Everyone	Year-End

Figure 6.8

At this point, the teacher and students need to consider a number of questions. What stories do they want to tell? What do they want their audience to know about students as learners? What outcomes would they like to result from their conferences? (See Example 6.7 and Blackline 6.11 at the end of this chapter.)

Schedule Conference—On Time

Students can be involved in setting up the schedule. For student-student conferences, cooperative groups can work to create schedules for in-school presentations. When parents or others are invited for conferences at specific times, students may talk with their parents to find out their best-available times. In planning for whole-class or schoolwide exhibitions, students can work within time allotments provided by teachers and administrators to plan the length of portfolio presentations.

Design Invitations—Invites

Once the conference dates have been scheduled, students will need to think about how they will invite their guests to portfolio conferences. Carefully designed invitations should tell guests the purpose and theme of the conference, exhibition, or Web showcase. Students should be involved in the design of brief, informal invitations. Alternatively, students can write a formal letter that includes information on what the guests can expect and even provide suggestions for conference protocol. Teachers promote learner responsibility and autonomy when they encourage students to consider these questions and to implement a plan together.

Anticipate Scheduling Problems—Conference at Home

Sometimes parents cannot attend the official portfolio conferences because of scheduling conflicts. In these instances, teachers can send home the portfolios along with guideline sheets that describe how the parents can conduct the conference at home. Web showcases can be presented at any time, of course, but teachers will want to know when parents are able to participate so guidelines for review can be e-mailed. Sometimes teachers will include sample questions to help parents or significant others start the process, as well as a form for them to record their feelings and impressions about the portfolio and the student's performance during the conference, or to give feedback on specific portfolio entries.

Determine Setup Blueprints

Students should be involved in planning how to arrange the room or a series of the rooms that will be needed for portfolio conferences or exhibitions. Students should create blueprints for display tables that will showcase artifacts from portfolios or other products and projects. They should also create posters or signs to direct guests from the entry doors to the conferences or exhibitions.

Conduct an Audience Audit—Know Your Audience

Just as the artist or the performer seeks out an audience to view and value the work completed, students must know who their audience will be and then plan to meet the expectations of this audience. Whether it's a peer conference, a teacher–school counselor–student conference, or a student-led parent conference, they need to think about what the audience will be looking for and how they can best highlight those things. The audience audit in Figure 6.9 will prepare students and teachers for the conference.

Choose Introductions—Introducing, Initiating, and Responding

If students are planning conferences for the first time, they may need some guidance in considering how they will introduce their portfolios, how they will initiate the communication with their audience, and how they might respond

Audience Audit	
Possible Audiences	**Probable Focus**
• Peers • Teacher • Guidance counselor • Parent(s)	• Academic pride, talents, and skills • Evidence of required work, meeting the standards • Areas of strength and weakness • Areas of progress and growth

Figure 6.9

to unanticipated comments or questions. By prompting student thinking about these social skills, teachers can ensure that each student will have the opportunity to practice or role-play some typical or atypical scenarios that may occur in parent-student or significant-other student conferences.

Set Protocol—Conference Etiquette

Students may need help to establish some conference guidelines or protocol for the benefit of their audiences. Again, the more autonomy students are given to prepare their portfolios and conference formats (within the established purposes), the more likely they will be to accept and maintain ownership of their learning processes. (For a sample protocol, see Example 6.10 at the end of this chapter.)

Design Questions—The Million-Dollar Question

The questions asked at conferences will vary depending on the type and purpose of the portfolios and the audience. Different questions target different conference goals. Figure 6.10 provides sample questions for four types of portfolio conferences.

Students and teachers also need to choose the nature of reflections they will use throughout the conference. What reflections do learners need to engage in? Should they prepare reflective questions or stem statements for their audience?

Honor a Time Frame—"Hang the Time Frame"

Everybody has experienced a presentation that drones on for too long. To avoid a boring presentation, students need to refocus. The portfolio speaks for itself in many ways, but the speaker needs to bring the overall portfolio alive. Care must be taken to target, rehearse, and actually present the portfolio within a predetermined time frame. "Hang the time frame" is a simple strategy for keeping students on track. Students hang up a sign that gives the allotted time. Like a cue card, the sign reminds the student presenter to be succinct and brief. Once the time frame is hung, a peer can audit the time for a partner as he or she practices the presentation. Practicing with this time frame technique provides a great opportunity to hone skills and develop desired emphasis.

Sample Questions for Four Types of Portfolio Conferences

Goal-Setting Conference	Student-Teacher Conference
Type: Single learning process (e.g., reading)	Type: Personally satisfying entries
1. How do you want to grow as a reader? 2. What strategies will you work to improve? 3. What are your goals for the next quarter? 4. How do you plan to achieve these goals?	1. Select one of the items in your portfolio and tell why you selected it. 2. Do you notice a pattern in the types of entries you like the best? Explain. 3. If you had included your least satisfying pieces, what would they be and why? 4. If you could show one entry to anyone, living or dead, who would it be?

Student-Led Parent-Teacher Conference	Student-Student Conference
Type: Significant achievement	Type: Group work
1. Explain why you included some of these items. 2. In what area have you achieved the greatest improvement? 3. Why do you think you have improved so much? 4. Which one of your achievements surprises you the most? Why? 5. How have you met the standards?	1. How do you feel about working in groups? 2. What was the biggest challenge of group work? 3. On which project or performance did your group do the best? Why? 4. If you could redo any group project, what would it be and why would you redo it? 5. What social skill do you want to work on?

Figure 6.10

Pick the Medium—Media Event

As portfolio conferences and exhibitions continue to incorporate technology, students become creative with media. Which medium will be used in the presentation? Will a computer slide show, film, video, or audiotape be used? Will the presentation be multimedia? If the answer to any of these options is "yes," the presenter must attend to media logistics. Students need to plan the elements for their multimedia presentation, or disaster may follow. The plus, minus, or interesting (PMI) strategy of de Bono (1992) may help students decide which media to include in their presentations (Figure 6.11).

By appraising the pluses (P), minuses (M), and interesting (I) aspects of a media presentation, students can have a better idea of what they may need to plan for in their own media presentation.

PMI Chart: Using Media in a Presentation

Record the Pluses, Minuses, and Interesting aspects in the chart below.

PLUS	
MINUS	
INTERESTING	

Figure 6.11

(Created by de Bono)

Show Personality—What's Your Style?

Students must choose a personal style for the portfolio presentation. Personal style involves how students present themselves in public and private situations. Some students prefer a lighthearted approach, using humor to defuse the tension that is part of any formal gathering. Others may be more comfortable presenting in a genuine, folksy way, sprinkling the presentation with personal anecdotes. Others may choose a reserved style, relying on the strength of the portfolio to "carry the show." Some may select a direct approach to the presentation, dotting the monologue with pointed questions. Students should question their own style. One way to discover one's best style is to videotape a rehearsal of the portfolio presentation for the student to analyze and reflect on. Another way is to have students work with partners and assess each other's style through peer dialogue.

Create Openings and Closings—Gotcha

A presenter makes or breaks a presentation in the first ninety seconds. Teachers can help students see the importance of the opening and the first artifacts shown. A good close leaves the audience feeling positive. Strong openings and closings involve the same elements: surprise, design, questions, mystery items, anecdotes, cartoons, quotes, graphics, questions, and skits. Students should be coached in choosing effective openings and closings for their portfolio conferences.

Rehearse Conference Dialogue—The Rehearsal

Before the conference, it is wise to conduct a "full dress rehearsal." This will help students overcome their nervousness and offer them a chance to fine-tune their presentations. Teachers can ask students to run through their presentations in pairs or groups. While a student practices his or her presentation, another student or students take on the role of the teacher, parent, or other interested audience member. Figures 6.12 and 6.13 are two sample dialogues to use as models. (See Blackline 6.12 at the end of this chapter.)

Sample Dialogue for a Student-Led Parent-Teacher Conference

Significant Achievement Portfolio

Student: Let me begin my portfolio conference by telling you a little bit about our portfolios and what the purpose has been since we began using them. Then I want you to look over some parts of it and have you ask me anything you would like.

Parent: All right. That sounds great.

Student: We use portfolios at this school because there are so many things that we are interested in learning that they can't all be shown by the tests we take.

Parent: Excuse me, you mean you don't use your tests for grades any more?

Student: (laughing) I wish! No, you'll see tests in my portfolio that are graded. Getting back to the purpose, we agreed that our portfolios would show us and you that we are learning important things in science, math, social studies, and other subjects. We're learning how to solve problems, to write about things that are important to us, and to become better at working on big projects or ideas together. So our portfolios are about our achievement in all our subjects but also about who we are as people. For this conference, we decided that we would choose pieces from our whole portfolio that show significant achievement.

Parent: These are things you got your best grades on?

Student: Not always, but most of the time. Let me show you this math paper (takes a paper from folder). I selected this one and wrote my reasons here. Do you want to read it?

Parent: Yes. (Reads, then looks at math paper.) So you figured out how to do this kind of problem, even though you got many problems wrong on the quiz.

Student: Yeah. It was when we were going over our mistakes in peer study groups that I figured it out. It was a great feeling!

Parent: I'm jealous. I wish that would have happened to me in algebra.

Student: Hey, I just got what it takes! (laughs) Anyway, all the rest of the things in my portfolio are like this. They show what I've learned, but they also show how and sometimes why. Let's look at some other pieces, and you can ask me whatever you want to know.

The teacher participated as an observer, stopped to greet the conference attendees, listened briefly to the discussion, and urged them to continue unless they had questions.

Figure 6.12

Sample Dialogue for a Teacher-Student Portfolio Conference

Personally Satisfying Portfolio

Teacher: I see you're ready to begin your portfolio conference. I'm impressed already. Your cover is great!

Student: Thanks! I got a little carried away, but I like the way it looks. It's really cool.

Teacher: Tell me about it, and then let's talk about what's inside.

Student: Well, since this was our personally satisfying portfolio conference, I got to wondering: If I got an award for each best work that was one of my favorite things, what would each award be?

Teacher: I like that idea.

Student: So, I glued on the ticket stubs from the baseball game my dad took us to, and then a card of my favorite player. Here's a picture of my favorite dessert—yes, chocolate! Here's a picture from my favorite vacation. And there's a whole bunch of other stuff that I love.

Teacher: This is fun to look at. Let's see what you've put inside.

Student: (apologetic) Well, it was hard to choose work from my working portfolio that was my best, because my opinion changes.

Teacher: I'm glad you noted that. I like that you did include this writing assignment from September. It was very good.

Student: Thanks, I know it was the best. It makes me feel good to look at it now because I remember working hard on it with the computer. It's easier for me to write when I type instead of writing with a pen or pencil. It looks better when it's done.

Teacher: Don't give up on your handwriting. It gets better all the time. Can you show me a piece that you think shows work on learning an idea or about an important issue or event that was satisfying to you?

Student: (thinking) Yes. I'll show you the science presentation that I did with my group. You remember . . . .

Figure 6.13

Plan the Postconference Evaluation—So What?

As the planning for the portfolio conference comes to a close and the day of the event approaches, it is important for students to think ahead to the "so what" of the conferences. How will they know if they have met their goals? How do they wish to evaluate the conferences? What would they like to learn by the end of the conference? What will be valued? The teacher will want to show the students a variety of evaluation ideas, including the possibility of preparing surveys or informal stem statements that request feedback from those who have had conferences with them. Students will be eager to share their experiences and to find out what their audience said about their portfolios. Both the teacher and the student participate in the postconference evaluation. (See Example 6.8 and Blackline 6.14 at the end of this chapter.)

In the same way that it is important to engage students in the reflection and processing of important learning experiences in the classroom, the individual student needs to self-assess the outcome of the portfolio conference, exhibition, or showcase. Whether a teacher has developed a scoring rubric or a reflection log for the event, the conference evaluation completed by the student must be seen as an important part of the portfolio connection process. Teachers can assist students in reviewing their purposes and objectives, analyzing the data they collected from the audience evaluations, and reflecting on the comments and suggestions they received during the conferences. In addition, students can assess the social skills and habits of mind that they used during the event. This ensures that each student has the opportunity to reflect on the pluses and minuses, while setting goals for future portfolio conferences, exhibitions, and showcases.

Examples

Short- and Long-Term Performance Goals

Name: ___Chris___   Term: ___2nd___

Subject: ___Social Studies Term Project___   Date: ___January 4___

Short-Term Goals	Target Date
1. Select project topic early.	January 10
2. Get to the library.	January 15
3. Create and use an outline.	January 30
4. Work with a partner to research online.	February 1

Long-Term Goals	Target Date
1. Include an interview with expert.	March 1
2. Read five historical fiction books on the topic.	March 30
3. Complete final project on time.	April 15

Date of Next Conference: ___Feb 3___

Comment: ___I won't procrastinate on this project like I did the last time.___

Typical Student Reflections on the Portfolio

I selected this photo because it has my book report in it and I am proud of my work. It is importa-t because I made it and I like my work. The activity in this picture is about me standing and holding my book report. I learned how to make a book float. I didn't have any problems. I would definately do it again and I wouldent chane a thing.

Example 6.1

Sample Dialogue for a Student-Led Parent-Teacher Conference

Significant Achievement Portfolio

Student: Let me begin my portfolio conference by telling you a little bit about our portfolios and what the purpose has been since we began using them. Then I want you to look over some parts of it and have you ask me anything you would like.

Parent: All right. That sounds great.

Student: We use portfolios at this school because there are so many things that we are interested in learning that they all can't be shown by the tests we take.

Parent: Excuse me, you mean you don't use your tests for grades anymore.

Student: (laughing) I wish! No, you'll see tests in my portfolio that are graded. Getting back to the purpose, we agreed that our portfolios would show us and you that we are learning important things in science, math, social studies, and other things. We're learning how to solve problems, to write about things that are important to us, and to become better at working on big projects or ideas together. So our portfolios are about our achievement in all our subjects but also about who we are as people. For this conference, we decided that we would choose pieces from our whole portfolio that show significant achievement.

Parent: These are things you got your best grades on?

Student: Not always, but most of the time. Let me show you this math paper (takes a paper from folder). I selected this one and wrote my reasons here. Do you want to read it?

Parent: Yes. (Reads, then looks at math paper.) So you figured out how to do this kind of problem, even though you got many problems wrong on the quiz.

Student: Yeah. It was when we were going over our mistakes in peer study groups that I figured it out. It was a great feeling!

Parent: I'm jealous. I wish that would have happened to me in algebra.

Student: Hey, I just got what it takes! (laughs) Anyway, all the rest of the things in my portfolio are like this. They show what I've learned, but they also show how and sometimes why. Let's look at some other pieces, and you can ask me whatever you want to know.

The teacher participated as an observer, stopped to greet the conference attendees, listened briefly to the discussion, and urged them to continue unless they had questions.

Example 6.2

Plugging in the Portfolio

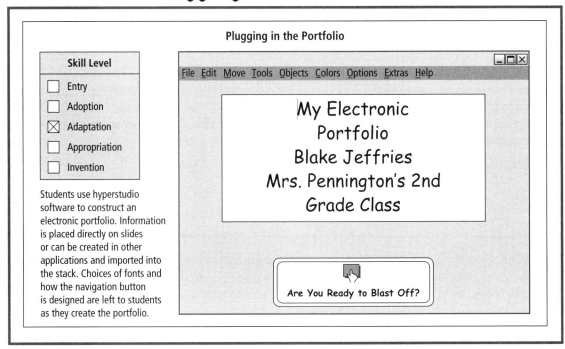

Example 6.3

Postconference Evaluation

Student Name: _Brian__ Grade Level: _8__

Conference Date: __11-14___

1. What were your goals?
   To share my portfolio with my parents.

2. List the goals you achieved.
   Covered all items. Answered their questions.

3. How do you feel about the conference(s)?
   Great! It's over!

4. Think of one suggestion you received during a conference that you know you want to try.
   More artwork.

5. Rate your overall portfolio conference(s).

   |—————————————|————————————————⊕——|

   Not Yet   Pretty Good   Yes! Yes! Yes!

Example 6.4

Portfolio Reflection Questions for Partners to Ask

Use this form as your partners share their e-portfolios. Write down their answers as best you can so they can place them in their folders.

If you were a teacher, the artifact with which you would be most impressed is _My report on the California Rivers_ because _I had many great pictures that I imported from the Internet. I also liked doing the free-hand drawings and the using pastel paints to color them._

What do you think is the most important characteristic of learning that your portfolio showcases?

I think this e-portfolio shows that I have been really good at finding good Internet resources for the information so it shows that I am using technology. I also think it shows that I am taking more pride in my work and that I am a good artist.

I think you could make a stronger case for meeting _the standard_ by reflecting on the last lab journal.

Maybe you are right about the science lab journals. I really like science but I have trouble using the format that Ms. Jones wants us to learn. I guess my lab journal is good but I never feel like I am that great in doing it. But I am glad that you feel I did a good job on this!

The most impressive part of your portfolio is

My entire e-portfolio was fun to create. I loved learning about bookmarks and hyperlinks. And I also liked adding my digital pictures of language arts projects to it. I feel like it really tells the story of who I am.

Example 6.5

NOTE: When completed, give this form to your partner, who will place it in his or her portfolio.

Choose Conference Goals

PORTFOLIO CONFERENCE GOALS SET BY STUDENTS

Primary

I want my portfolio to tell my story about how I learned to read this year.

Intermediate

By the time my parents are done looking at my portfolio and talking to me about my work and the reflections I have written, I want them to be as excited as I am about how much I have improved in everything!

High School

My portfolio conference should show the teachers in this school that I have really learned how to use computers to organize and present a project on communications.

Example 6.6

Set Protocol

PORTFOLIO CONFERENCE PROTOCOL FOR AUDIENCES

The following are some tips that the students from our school have designed to help you get the most from your portfolio conference. We hope you enjoy visiting with our students.

- Listen to the student.
- If responses are unclear, please ask for more information.
- Concentrate on one piece at a time.
- Make comments about the portfolios that can help students to look at their work from new perspectives or to value their work from another person's view.
- Ask students to tell you how they feel about their work at Washington Elementary.
- Ask if students need any help meeting standards.

Example 6.7

Student-Led Conference Checklist

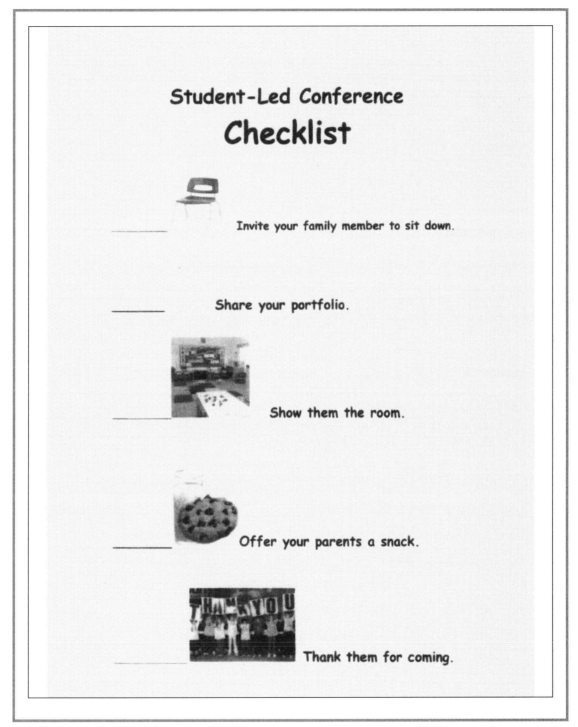

Example 6.8

Used with permission from Julie Fabrocini.

Student-Led Conference Etiquette

This is a wonderful opportunity for you to enjoy your child as he or she makes a formal presentation showcasing learning goals and explaining samples of completed work. Remember, if you would like to meet with us (your child's teachers) we are always available to have a team meeting to discuss your child's progress. This time, however, has been set aside for your child to lead.

LISTEN CAREFULLY

Your child has planned this conference and wants to show you what he or she has learned.

LOOK FOR GROWTH

Your child has been learning to be a self-directed learner and needs encouragement.

ASK QUESTIONS, but remember, interruptions may break your child's concentration.

OFFER SUPPORT

Your child will appreciate your willingness to support learning goals. We appreciate your participation today and encourage you to fill out the evaluations at the end of the conference while this experience is still fresh in your mind. Thank you for your support!

The Teachers and Staff at Chime Charter School

Example 6.9

Used with permission from Julie Fabrocini.

Postconference Feedback Sheet

Please complete at the conclusion of your conference. Place sheet in portfolio folder and return it to us before you leave tonight.

What aspects of the Student-Led Conference were the most positive for you?

_____

_____

_____

What aspects of the Student-Led Conference were the most positive aspects for your child?

_____

_____

_____

What aspects of the Student-Led Conferences were the least positive for you or your child?

_____

_____

_____

Please cite any observations regarding your child's growth as reflected in the conference or portfolios.

_____

_____

_____

Would you like to see this format continued in the future? Yes No If no, please explain

_____

_____

_____

Do you have any recommendations for improvement of the student-led conferences?

_____

_____

_____

Additional comments:

_____

_____

_____

Thank you for taking the time to attend this conference and completing this feedback form.

Example 6.10

Used with permission from Julie Fabrocini.

Parent Response Sheet for Portfolio Review

Parent Response Sheet for Portfolio Review

Name _____   Date _____

Two Stars

One Wish

Example 6.11

Used with permission from Julie Fabrocini.

Blacklines

Exhibit Your Work

Student Name: _____

Directions to Student: Think about each element and jot down your thoughts.

Scoring the Goal:

Audience Audit:

Hang the Time Frame:

Media Event:

What's Your Style?

Gotcha (Openings/Closings):

Blackline 6.1

Evaluation of Portfolio Conference

Student Name: _____   Grade: _____

Conference Date: _____

What were your goals for this conference? _____

_____

_____

_____

List the goals you achieved. _____

_____

_____

_____

How do you feel about the conference? _____

_____

_____

_____

List at least one suggestion you received during the conference that you want to try at the next conference.

_____

_____

_____

Rate your overall portfolio conference using the ratings below.

|————————————|————————————|————————————|————————————|————————————|
Not Yet   Getting Started   Pretty Good   Almost There   Yes! Yes! Yes!

Blackline 6.2

Strategic Plan

Directions: In the boxes provided, write the specific steps or actions needed to reach your goal. Remember to include time frames or dates.

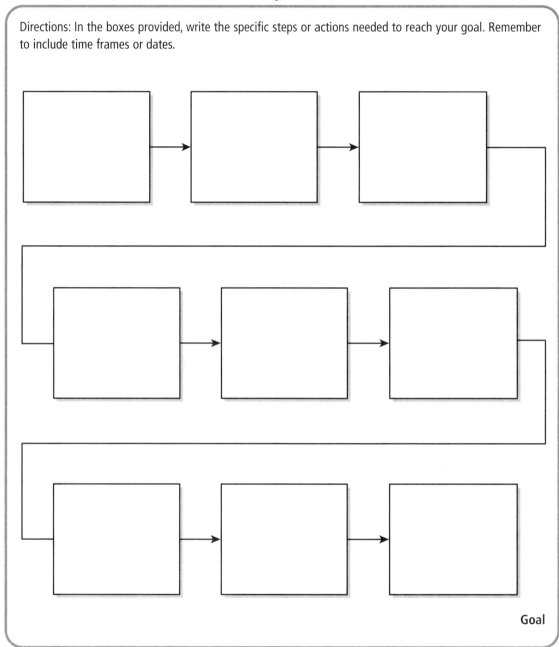

Goal

Blackline 6.3

Peer Reflections on Portfolios

If I were a teacher, the artifact with which I would be most impressed is _____
_____ because

_____

_____

_____

_____

What is the most important characteristic of your learning that you think your portfolio showcases?

_____

_____

_____

_____

I think you could make a stronger case for meeting _____ by reflecting on the _____ item that you included.

_____

_____

_____

_____

The most impressive part of your portfolio is

_____

_____

_____

_____

Blackline 6.4

NOTE: When completed, give this form to your partner, who will place it in his or her portfolio.

Student-Led Portfolio Conference Welcome

I want you to know that I love it when . . .

In school I get excited about . . .

My favorite activity is . . .

I am best at . . .

I need to improve . . .

You can help me by . . .

Blackline 6.5

Reflective Questions for Student Portfolios

These are sample questions that students can ask themselves when preparing for the portfolio conference or e-portfolio showcase.

1. Why have I chosen this piece?

2. What are its strengths? weaknesses?

3. Why is it important?

4. How and where does it fit in with what I already know?

5. What category does it fit into?

6. How might I label it appropriately?

7. What if I took it out of my portfolio?

8. How do I think others will react to it?

9. On a scale of 1–10, I give it a _____ because _____.

10. What question might someone ask me about this item?

11. How do I really feel about this?

12. Does this piece meet the standards?

Blackline 6.6

Reflective Questions

Entry Selection and Creation

Select One Entry: _____

1. What standard did you meet?

2. What process did you use to complete the entry?

3. What problems did you encounter?

4. How did you solve those problems?

5. What did you learn by doing this entry?

6. What would you do differently if you did it again?

Signed: _____   Date: _____

           (student)

Blackline 6.7

Sample Student Reflection Statements for Portfolios

This is my favorite piece because . . .

I'll remember this piece twenty years from now because . . .

If I could do this piece over again, I would . . .

This piece will surprise many people because . . .

My parent(s) liked this piece because . . .

This piece was my greatest challenge because . . .

This piece shows I met standard #_____ because . . .

This piece is my favorite/least favorite because . . .

Blackline 6.8

Teacher Planner for Portfolio Conferences

Who will participate?

_____

_____

_____

What type of portfolio conference will be planned?

_____

_____

_____

What are the goals of the conference?

_____

_____

_____

What are the logistics?

Date: _____ Time: _____ Place: _____

Invitations: _____

_____

Room setup: _____

_____

Refreshments: _____

_____

How will you evaluate the conferences?

_____

_____

_____

Blackline 6.9

The Web Showcase Plan

Student Name: _____

Directions to Student: Think about each element and jot down your thoughts.

Scoring the Goal:

Audience Audit:

Hang the Time Frame:

Media Event:

What's Your Style?

Gotcha (Openings/Closings):

Blackline 6.10

Teacher Planner Checklist for Exhibitions

❑ Date _____   ❑ Time _____

❑ Place

_____

_____

_____

❑ Invitations

_____

_____

_____

❑ Refreshments

_____

_____

_____

❑ Equipment

_____

_____

_____

Blackline 6.11

Peer Reflections on Portfolios

If I were a teacher, the artifact with which I would be most impressed is _____

_____ because

_____

_____

_____

_____

What is the most important characteristic of your learning that you think your portfolio showcases?

_____

_____

_____

_____

I think you could make a stronger case for meeting _____ by reflecting on the _____ item that you included.

_____

_____

_____

_____

The most impressive part of your portfolio is

_____

_____

_____

_____

Blackline 6.12

NOTE: When completed, give this form to your partner, who will place it in his or her portfolio.

Teacher Planner: Metacognitive Reflection

Think about each of these reflective tools and jot down one way you might use each of them with your students as they learn to plan, monitor, and evaluate their portfolio work.

Planning

Visualization

_____

_____

Strategic Planning

_____

_____

Establishing Benchmarks

_____

_____

Monitoring

Labeling

_____

_____

Bridging Questions

_____

_____

Evaluating

Artifact Registry

_____

_____

Anecdotes

_____

_____

Blackline 6.13

Parent Web Showcase/Conference Guide

Dear Parent: Please review your son's/daughter's portfolio and ask questions about his or her work. The following questions might help start the discussion. Thank you for your cooperation.

1. What have you learned about yourself by putting together your portfolio?

2. What is your favorite piece? Why?

3. If you could publish one thing in this portfolio, what would it be and why?

4. Select one item and tell how you feel about it.

Please write any comments you have and give this sheet to your son/daughter to return to school.

_____

_____

_____

_____

_____

Signed: _____ Date: _____

Blackline 6.14

Conference Map

- What will the goals be?

- Is the presentation for a peer conference or for a student-led parent conference?

- Is the presentation for a class exhibition or for a schoolwide portfolio showcase?

- What reflections do learners need to engage in?

- Will students need to compare their achievement to benchmarks and learning standards?

- Will the portfolio need to show progress over time?

- Will it show achievement of individual learning goals?

- What questions should learners prepare for their audience?

- Who is the audience?

- What are they looking for?

- How are they going to view the work?

- Are they familiar with the type of work?

- What can be done to maximize the audience's interest and understanding?

- How do they wish to evaluate the conferences?

- Is there a particular format and scoring rubric to follow?

- Will they evaluate the contents and the reflections?

- Will they focus on social skills and communication?

- Will they evaluate the audience's reaction to what they learned about the students as readers, writers, thinkers, problem solvers, etc.?

Blackline 6.15

Conclusion

In June 2007, the Association for Supervision and Curriculum Development (ASCD) launched their *Campaign for Whole Child Education.* The Association, "called upon parents, educators, policy makers, and communities to join forces to ensure our children become productive, engaged citizens. Our children deserve an education that emphasizes academic rigor as well as the essential 21st-century skills of critical thinking and creativity" (ASCD 2007). As we have stressed throughout each of the editions of *The Portfolio Connection,* educators and policymakers need to place all students and their families at the center of curriculum and assessment. We agree with the ASCD position: "At a time of rapid change and innovation, our education system is struggling to keep pace with this dynamic, digital world. Too often, young people are asked to learn 21st-century skills with 20th-century tools. While the demands for a highly skilled and educated workforce are growing. . . . the alarming fact is that we are still losing too many kids and wasting too much talent" (ASCD 2007). We agree with the ASCD position that teachers must be empowered to provide students with "evidence-based" assessment and instructional practices that are critical for continuing progress in closing the achievement gap.

Throughout the third edition of *The Portfolio Connection,* we have presented ways in which educators might create portfolios and e-portfolios with clear purposes and comprehensible procedures for promoting student motivation and voice throughout their PreK–12 education. The book provides useful tools for students to collect significant work samples over time, store them efficiently, and ultimately select them as the messages about themselves that they believe will tell the important and "whole" story of their talents, learning, and achievement. Student "voice" has been emphasized throughout this edition because we recognize that it has become silenced during a period of distinct reliance on high-stakes testing. As has been stressed in the book, academic portfolios and e-portfolios serve educators and students as containers of assessment for learning where each student is placed at the center of the learning experience.

The increasingly important use of the PreK–12 student e-portfolio as a more systematic and efficient evidence-collection tool has been presented throughout the book. While the e-portfolio development process in many ways parallels the traditional portfolio, it has become clear that its distinct properties can address many more purposes and audiences. We have presented procedures and tools for educators to use in aligning both the portfolio and e-portfolio process with national expectations for successful achievement of learning objectives and standards for all students. Rather than a narrow lens that focuses on assessment *of* student learning, however, the development of the portfolio continues to be positioned in a way that represents formative assessment *for* student learning.

While the academic portfolio held great promise two decades ago as an important, student-centered means to promote the important connection between PreK–12 students and their audience of peers, teachers, parents administrators, and "critical others," the implementation of the No Child Left Behind legislation has presented sizable challenges to the continued promotion of student voice in the learning process. High-stakes testing accompanied by a high degree of pressure for accountability of classroom teachers, schools, school districts, and states has resulted in an all-consuming focus on "teaching to the test" (Popham 2003) and the near-abandonment of student-centered processes of learning and self-assessment in schools. We offer this edition of *The Portfolio Connection* as both a tool kit and road map for educators who wish to return to curriculum and assessment that promotes education and development of all students' minds, skills, character, and knowledge. The ASCD *Campaign for Whole Child Education* affirms this goal:

> Participatory democracy hinges on a social compact between adults and children that we shall together prepare them for a brighter future. For too long we have maintained a status quo in education that has at best prepared children for our past and at worst marginalized those families least able to access a better life for their children through means other than education. We have been committed to time structures, coursework, instructional methods and assessments that do not reveal to our children the marvel that they are and instead often leave them questioning their worth and the purpose of education designed more than a century ago. It is time to put the students at the center of the education system and align resources to their multiple needs to ensure a balanced education for all. (ASCD, 2007, p. 5)

Appendix

Photo used with permission from Sarah Belgrad

GREEK MYTHOLOGY UNIT

My Portfolio

Table of Contents

LANGUAGE ARTS

"THE FIRST SUPER BOWL ON MT. OLYMPUS"

There once was a football coach named Zeus
Whose sportsmanship and morals were loose
He would lie and he'd cheat
Every team he would meet
Until Athena would call a truce.

The Greek Gods of Old Olympic High
Were conceited and quick with a lie
They'd toy with mortal men
In vain attempts to win
And on gold winged sandals they would fly.

Poseidon charged with trident in hand
Chased by the Olympus Marching Band
The next one to follow
Was Captain Apollo
Selling his newest sun lotion brand.

The mortal Greeks in the scrimmage fell
And were cast by Hades into hell
They soon began to plot
And place kicked a lot
And formed their own league—The NFL.

Reflection:
I really enjoy writing poetry
—especially funny poems. I
try to use rhyming words
that are interesting. It's hard
with limericks because you
have to have three words
that rhyme. I'd like to write
jingles for ads on television
someday. I don't know
what other jobs require
poetry writing.

The Greeks took the field for the final game
To crush the Gods was the mortals' aim
The Gods endured the boos
The Greeks wore Nike shoes
The first Super Bowl brought the Greeks fame!
—Sarah Medusa

My Best Piece!

1

Standard: Students will produce writings from a variety of genres.

BIOGRAPHY OF A WORK

ITEM: LIMERICK—THE FIRST SUPER BOWL ON MT. OLYMPUS

Date	Summary
9/17	Teacher assigned a poem about Greek mythology. We could choose any type of poetry we wanted.
9/19	I started writing about the first pep rally at Olympus High using aabb rhyme scheme. Frustrating!
9/21	Didn't like the poem—It was too "sing-songy." Decided to change to limerick with aabba rhyme scheme.
9/23	Wrote five drafts of poems. Used ˘ / ˘ / ˘ / ˘ / ˘ / symbols to count syllables in each line to make sure I had 9-9-6-6-9 in each line. Very time consuming!
9/25	Typed poem on computer and cut out pictures to put on it. Wish I could draw better.
9/27	Read poem to the class and they thought it was awesome! The class wants to make it into a skit to show at the exhibition.
Reflection	
I think this poem is one of my best pieces. It's funny, creative, and it shows how much I know about the gods and goddesses. It also shows that I know how to write limericks—and they are not easy!	

2

PHYSICAL EDUCATION

GROUP PROJECT OF OLYMPIC GAMES

Our group selected events used in the Greek Olympics and demonstrated what the events looked like. We selected the 10-meter race and discus throw and took a video of what the events looked like (video in portfolio).

Of course, I had to pretend I was a boy because girls did not participate in the early Olympics and they were not allowed to attend.

> **Reflection:** This is not our best work. The filming of the video was difficult because we didn't use a tripod. The camera moves around too much and is sometimes out of focus. We need to learn how to edit a video. Also, our script wasn't very good. Our narrator ran out of things to say!

3

Standard: Students will integrate technology into presentations.

SOURCE: Photo used with permission from Sarah Belgrad

THE MODERN-DAY LABORS OF HERCULES

Hercules was a Greek hero who was hated by Hera. Hera made Hercules go crazy, and in a fit of rage he killed his wife and children. The famous 12 labors he was forced to perform were a penalty for his crimes. If Hercules were alive today, the following "Herculean tasks" could be assigned to him by Hera:

Labor 1:   Make Hermes, the god of magic, reduce the U.S. deficit.

Labor 2:   Bring back Elvis from the rock-and-roll underworld.

Labor 3:   Reduce the Hydra-headed evils of drugs and violence in our cities.

Labor 4:   Clean out the Augean sewers of New York.

Labor 5:   Wrestle the god San Andreas and tie him down to prevent more earthquakes along the fault line in California.

Labor 6:   Capture the winds of Aeolus in a bag to prevent hurricanes from hitting Florida.

Labor 7:   Bring back the head of Medusa, the goddess whose looks turn men to stone.

Labor 8:   Wrestle the evil Hulk Hogan in the land of Wrestlemania.

Labor 9:   Capture the evil Harpie Sisters and cancel their syndicated talk show.

Labor 10: Fight the three-headed monster Barney, who guards the entrance to "Toys R Us."

Labor 11: Harness the fire-breathing reindeer of "Santataur" from the land of the North Pole and make them bring the chariot of gifts to our school.

Labor 12: Level the plains of Woodstock and sow salt so that no music festival can "spring from the earth" again.

Reflection: I'm not too happy with this piece. At first I was going to be serious and have the modern-day Hercules conquer real problems. Then I tried to be humorous. I think I ended up somewhere in between. Should have added more artwork to this piece.

Standard: Students will analyze literary works.

SCIENCE

ORIGINAL MYTH TO EXPLAIN

"How We Got Lightning Bugs"

There once was a snotty Greek youth named Bugga. He was always playing practical tricks on people. He would sneak around during the night at drive-ins and flatten chariot wheels of couples who were kissing. He used to sneak up on the mortals and the gods in the dark and pull his childish pranks.

One day, however, Bugga played a trick on the wrong god. Bugga was sitting behind the stables of Mt. Olympus one night watching the nymphs prepare Apollo's horses to drive the sun chariot to bring up the sun for the new day. While no one was looking, he placed tiny walkman transistors in the horses' ears. Apollo soon arrived at the stables in all his golden splendor. The sun god radiated fire and power as he boarded his chariot, hooked up the sun to the back end, and prepared to take his daily ride to bring up the sun for the world.

When he left the stable, the horses charged ahead wildly out of control. Apollo used all his godly powers to restrain them. For you see, Bugga had inserted *heavy metal* tapes into their walkmen, and the horses, crazy from the sound, were plunging toward earth and a fiery collision.

Apollo was finally able to control the fierce beasts and bring them and the sun back safely to Mt. Olympus. When he returned, he heard snickering coming from the bushes, and he uncovered Bugga laughing hysterically. Apollo realized the prank Bugga had played, and he knew he would have to punish the young punk for almost burning up the earth.

"Bugga, you think you're pretty cool, don't you?" whispered Apollo.

"What, old dude, I don't know what you're talking about," Bugga whined.

"You won't be sneaking around in the dark anymore to play your tricks. Everyone will know when you are around."

With that comment, Apollo struck Bugga with his lyre, and Bugga shrunk to a small flying bug. Apollo touched the bug again, and this time Bugga's tail lit up.

"Now," laughed Apollo, "try to sneak around at night. Your glow will give you away. People will capture you in their hands and imprison you in jars. You'll be a firefly! And since you like that horrible heavy metal music so much, I'll curse you so you can never hear again!"

And to this day whenever you see a firefly—it's really Bugga. But don't try to yell to him. He can't hear you!

Reflection: I need to work on my dialogue. It doesn't sound natural yet. I also want to edit this story. I tend to be too wordy. I think I can have the same effect by "tightening up" the story. I also need to work on the ending.

5

MATH

MATH PROBLEM USING PYTHAGOREAN THEOREM

Pythagoras was a Greek mathematician who was born around 500 B.C. He later founded a school to promote the study of natural science, philosophy, and mathematics. He is most famous for discovering the relationship beween the lengths of the sides of a right triangle. I can use this theorem to find unknown lengths of a triangle.

Pythagorean Theorem—In any right triangle with legs a and b, and hypotenuse c, $a^2 + b^2 = c^2$.

Problem: Find c, the length of the hypotenuse.

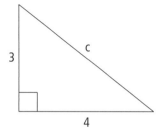

Solution:

$a^2 + \underline{b^2} = c^2$ Write the theorem.
$3^2 + 4^2 = c^2$ Substitute values for variables.
$9 + 16 = c^2$
$25 = c^2$
$\sqrt{25} = c$
$5 = c$

The hypotenuse, c, has a length of 5.

Check:

$a^2 + b^2 = c^2$ substitute values
$3^2 + 4^2 = 5^2$

Reflection: I'm still not too sure where I will ever use this in life. I will have to think of a word problem to write. I just know I can now verify right triangles and find missing values of right triangles.

$9 + 16 = 25$

$25 = 25$

6

ART

PRODUCTS FROM MYTHOLOGY

Ajax—Mighty Greek Warrior
and Sink Cleanser

Trident—Poseidon's
Symbol and Gum

Mars—Roman God of War
and Candy Bar

Midas—A King with the
Golden Touch and a
Muffler

Mt. Olympus—Palace of
Gods and Olympic-Sized
Swimming Pools

Titans—Original
Gods and Large
Ship (*Titanic*)

Helios—Sun God and
Helium Balloons

Reflection: I have trouble drawing people, but I have learned to draw simple things in my art class. I need to take more art courses.

THE TROJAN WAR
Venn Diagram Comparing the Greeks and Trojans

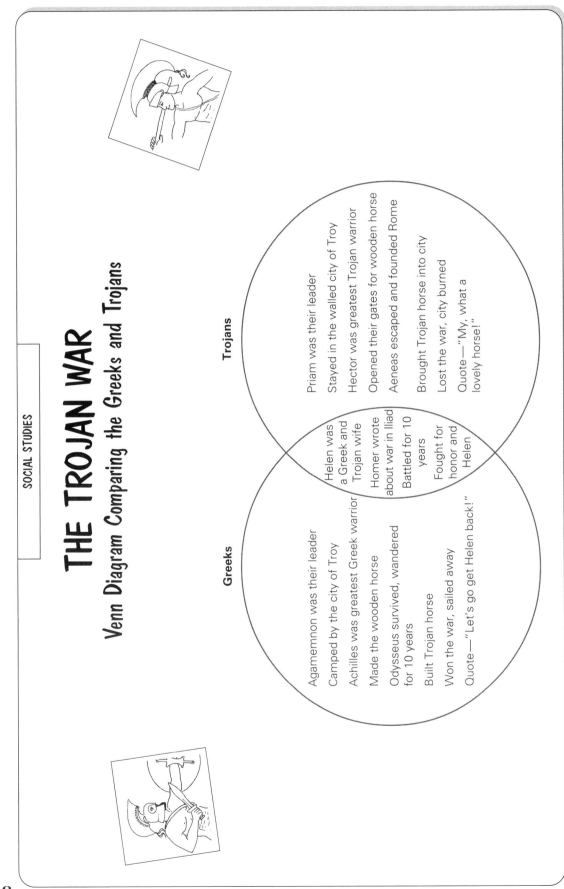

Greeks

Agamemnon was their leader

Camped by the city of Troy

Achilles was greatest Greek warrior

Made the wooden horse

Odysseus survived, wandered for 10 years

Built Trojan horse

Won the war, sailed away

Quote—"Let's go get Helen back!"

Helen was a Greek and Trojan wife

Homer wrote about war in Iliad

Battled for 10 years

Fought for honor and Helen

Trojans

Priam was their leader

Stayed in the walled city of Troy

Hector was greatest Trojan warrior

Opened their gates for wooden horse

Aeneas escaped and founded Rome

Brought Trojan horse into city

Lost the war, city burned

Quote—"My, what a lovely horse!"

Standard: Students will compare and contrast ideas.

238

PORTFOLIO RUBRIC

☑ Self   ☐ Peer   ☐ Teacher

	Hades	**Parthenon**	**Mt. Olympus**
	1	2	③
1. Creative cover	The Underworld Gazette	The Athens Chronicle	The Olympus Sun
	1	2	③
2. Completeness	Minotaur (half man, half bull)	Perseus (half man, half god)	Zeus (all god)
	1	②	3
3. Form (spelling, grammar, punctuation, sentence structure)	Dionysus (Sloppy—god of wine)	Odysseus (Needs help—phone home)	Hermes (Great—god of alphabet)
	1	②	3
4. Creativity	Touched by mere mortals	Touched by the demigods	Touched by the god of creativity
	1	2	③
5. Evidence of understanding	Hercules (Where are my Spark Notes?)	Apollo (I see the light)	Athena (goddess of wisdom)
	1	2	③
6. Reflection	Medusa (never uses a mirror)	Narcissus (gazes at own image only)	Aphrodite (reflects in mirror on regular basis)

Comments: I know I still need to work on my sentence structure—but sometimes it gets in the way of creativity. I really don't get grammar rules. "They're Greek to me!"

Total Points: 16 = A

Scale: Total 18 pts.
15 – 18 = A
10 – 14 = B
 6 – 9 = C
Below 6 = Not Yet

9

SELF-ASSESSMENT OF PORTFOLIO

STEM QUESTIONS

1. What is your favorite piece? Why?

My favorite piece is my limerick about the first Super Bowl on Mt. Olympus. I've always liked to write funny poems, but no one ever saw them. Now the whole class likes my poems. They've asked me to write a poem about our football team to read at the next pep rally. I'm really excited.

2. What piece is least satisfying to you? Why?

The group project where we videotaped some of the events from the Olympic Games. We weren't very organized and our camera work wasn't good. Sometimes it's harder to get things done right when five people have to agree. We need more team-building skills!

3. If you could share this portfolio with anyone living or dead, who would it be?

I would like to share my portfolio with my grandmother because she used to read me stories from a mythology book when I was young. I didn't like fairy tales as much as the stories of the gods and goddesses. I grew up loving Greek mythology and I'd like to share this portfolio with the person who inspired me.

10

GOAL-SETTING

MY SHORT-TERM GOALS

Goals	Target Date
1. I need to learn how to use spell check and grammar check on my computer.	Jan. 20
2. I need to find out how to write better reflections. Mine all say about the same thing.	March 6
3. I need to find out when I would use the Pythagorean theorem—I don't understand why it's important.	By next test

MY LONG-TERM GOALS

Goals	Target Date
1. I want to learn how to do more computer graphics to help the layout of my portfolio and my other work.	Jan. 27
2. I want to work on my group skills. I lost my patience with group members when we did our video.	Feb. 3
3. I would like to take some elective courses in creative writing.	1996

Date of next conference: _____*April 3*_____   Signed: _____*Medusa Sarah*_____

11

ARTIFACT REGISTRY

Student: _____Sarah_____   Grade: _____8th_____   Date: ___10/5___

DELETIONS

Date	Item	Reasons
10/5	Math problem using Pythagorean Theorem	I didn't understand when and why I would need to use this.
10/5	Group project of Olympic Games Video	Poor quality. Picture moved around. Bad sound. Lots of pauses.

ADDITIONS

Date	Item	Reasons
10/5	Word problem using Pythagorean Theorem	I wrote a problem about buying fencing for my yard. Made more sense.
10/5	Group video of interviews of athletes after races	We learned how to use camera better and we wrote a good script for interviewer and athletes.

12

QUESTIONS FOR PORTFOLIO CONFERENCE

Student: _____*Sarah*_____   Date: _____*Oct. 5*_____

I have prepared the following questions that peers, parents, or teachers could ask me about my portfolio during the conference.

1. If you could become one of the mortals or gods from Greek mythology, who would you become and why?

2. If you could select one item from this portfolio to share with the whole student body, what would it be and why?

3. What subject area do you think you need to work on most? Why?

4. What do you think was the major contribution the Greeks gave the world? Explain your answer.

5. If you could board a time machine and go back to 5th century Greece for a day to interview anyone, who would it be and why?

6. Compare the fall of Troy to the fall of the Roman Empire, fall of Germany, or fall of Saigon.

7. Explain this quotation: "Beware of Greeks bearing gifts."

8. If you lived in 5th century Greece, would you rather live in Athens or Sparta? Explain why.

9. Compare the work in this portfolio to the quizzes and tests you took on Greek mythology.

10. Which item in this portfolio was the most difficult for you to do? Why?

11. What are your goals for your next portfolio?

12. Which god or goddess from mythology would be considered the most "politically incorrect" if he or she lived today? Why?

13

EXHIBITION IDEAS FOR PORTFOLIO

Location: _____*School Gym*_____   Date: _____*Oct. 20*_____   Time: ___*10.00*___

Who's Invited *Other classes, administration, parents, community members* _____

Description: Students and teachers dress up as their favorite character from Greek mythology. The students display their portfolios on tables as well as artifacts (posters, games, projects) they have done. Visitors are invited to talk with students and visit the four corners of the gym.

Corner #1—Refreshments—students serve ambrosia (mixed fruit), nectar (fruit juice), and grapes (food of the gods).

Corner #2—Video Corner—where copies of students' video skits and performances are shown.

Corner #3—Sports Corner—students demonstrate the athletic events that were included in the Olympic Games.

Corner #4—Music Corner—students present music of the Greeks using harps, lyres, and flutes. Groups perform Greek rap songs.

Culminating Event: Class presents original skit from mythology to group.

14

References

Adelman, E. 1992. Portphotos: Using snapshots for portfolio assessment. Conference proceedings. Costa Del Sur Region 8 Language Arts Conference, Los Angeles, California, April 29, 1992.

Alaska Department of Education and Early Development. (1996). A collection of assessment strategies. www.eed.state.ak.us/tls/Frameworks/mathsci/ms5_ 2as1.htm.

American Educational Research Association. *AERA Position statement concerning high-stakes testing.* Retrieved November 12, 2007, from http://www.aera.net/policyand programs/?id=378 (Adopted, 2000).

Ash, L. E. (2000). *Electronic student portfolios.* Thousand Oaks, CA: Corwin Press.

Association for Supervision and Curriculum Development. *Campaign for Whole Child Education.* Retrieved August 3, 2007, from http://www.vaascd.org/WholeChildnews letter.fall.pdf.

Barrett, H. (2004a). Differentiating electronic portfolios and online assessment management systems. Proceedings of the 2004 Annual Conference of the Society for information Technology in Teacher Education. Atlanta, Georgia, March 2, 2004. http:// electronicportfolios.com/portfolios/SITE2004symp2.pdf.

Barrett, H. (2004b). Electronic portfolios as digital stories of deep learning. Retrieved June 10, 2007, from http:// electronicportfolios.com/digistory/epstory.html.

Barrett, H. (2005). One portfolio for life. *E-portfolios for learning.* Blog. Retrieved June 10, 2007, from http://electronic portfolios.org/blog/2005/07/one-portfolio-for-life.html.

Barrett, H. (2006). Researching electronic portfolios: Learning, engagement and collaboration through technology. *Technology Connected Newsletter* 1, 13, 2, 4–6.

Bass, H. (1993). Let's measure what's worth measuring. *Education Week, 32.*

Batson, T. (2002). The electronic portfolio boom: What's it all about? *Syllabus Online Magazine.* Richmond, VA: Virginia Community College Regional Centers for Excellence.

Bellanca, J. & Fogarty. R. (2003). *Blueprints for achievement in the cooperative* classroom (3rd ed.). Thousand Oaks, CA: Corwin Press.

Benson, B., & Barnett, S. (2005). *Student-led conferencing using showcase portfolios.* Thousand Oaks, CA: Corwin Press.

Bergmann, T. (2004). Feasible electronic portfolios: Global networking for the self-directed learner in the digital age. www.mehs.educ.state.ak.us/adstaff/bergman/bergman.htm

Bernhardt, V. L. (1994). *The school portfolio: A comprehensive framework for school improvement.* Princeton, NJ: Eye on Education.

Bostock, S. *Student peer assessment.* Retrieved May 28, 2006, from http://www.keele .ac.uk/depts/aa/landt/lt/docs/bostock_peer_assessment.htm.

Burke, K. 2005. *How to assess authentic learning* (4th ed.). Thousand Oaks, CA: Corwin Press.

Carr, J. E., & Harris, D. E. (2001). *Succeeding with standards: Linking curriculum, assessment, and action planning.* Alexandria, VA: Association for Supervision and Curriculum Development.

Catalyst. (2007). *Designing a portfolio.* Retrieved June 10, 2007, from catalyst.washington.edu/help/planning/portfolio_design.html.

Chapman, C. (1993). *If the shoe fits.* Thousand Oaks, CA: Corwin Press.

Cole, D. J., Ryan, C. W., Kick, E., & Mathies, B. K. (2000). *Portfolios across the curriculum and beyond* (2nd ed.). Thousand Oaks, CA: Corwin Press.

Committee on Technology, Communication, and Literacy. (2004). Call for proposals for the 50th annual convention. *International Reading Association.* Retrieved February, 2004 from http://www.reading.org.

Costa, A. L. (1991). *The school as a home for the mind.* Thousand Oaks, CA: Corwin Press.

Costa, A. L., & Kallick, B. (2000). *Habits of mind* (series of 4). Alexandria, VA: Association for Supervision and Curriculum Development.

Costa, A., & Kallick, B. (1992). Reassessing assessment. In A. L. Costa, J. A. Bellanca, & R. Fogarty (Eds.), *If minds matter: A foreword to the future,* Vol. II (pp. 275–280). Thousand Oaks, CA: Corwin Press.

Costa, A., & Kallick, B. (1995). *Assessment in the learning organization: Shifting the paradigm.* Alexandria, VA: Association for Supervision and Curriculum Development.

Costa, A. L. & Kallick, B. (2006). *Describing 16 habits of mind.* Retrieved May 28, 2006, from http://www.habits-of-mind.net/pdf/16HOM2.pdf.

Cox, K. (2007). Ms. Cox's pre-K class. www.prekinders.com.

Crafton, L. (1991). *Whole language: Getting started . . . moving forward.* Katonah, NY: Richard C. Owen.

Council for Exceptional Children. (2007). *New CEC policy on high stakes assessment.* Retrieved March 6, 2007 from http://www.cec.sped.org/Content/NavigationMenu/Publications2/CECToday/New_CEC_Policy_on_High_Stakes_Assessment.htm.

Crafton, L., & Burke, C. L. (1994, April). Inquiry-based evaluations: Teachers and students reflecting together. *Primary Voices,* 2–7.

Darling-Hammond, L., J. Ancess, B. Falk. 1995. Authentic assessment in action. *Studies of schools and students at work.* New York: Teachers College Press, Columbia University.

de Bono, E. (1992). *Serious creativity.* New York: HarperCollins.

*Dietz. (1992). Professional development portfolio. In *Frameworks.* Shoreham, NY: California Professional Development Program.

Flavell, J. H. (1976). Metacognitive aspects of problem solving. In L. B. Resnick (Ed.), *The nature of intelligence* (pp. 231–236). Hillsdale, NJ: Lawrence Erlbaum Associates.

Fogarty, R., & Stoehr, J. (1995). *Integrating the curricula with multiple intelligences: Teams, themes, and threads.* Thousand Oaks, CA: Corwin Press.

Gardner, H. (1983). *Frames of mind: The theory of multiple intelligences.* New York: HarperCollins.

Gardner, H. (1993). *Multiple intelligences: The theory in practice.* New York: HarperCollins.

Gergen, D. (2005). How to close the achievement gap today! *21st Century Schools Project Bulletin: PPI,* 5, 14.

Glazer, S. M. (1998). *Assessment is instruction: Reading, writing, spelling, and phonics for all learners.* Norwood, MA: Christopher-Gordon Publishers.

Guskey, T. R., & Bailey, J. M. (2001). *Developing grading and reporting systems for student learning.* Thousand Oaks, CA: Corwin Press.

Harste, J., V. Woodward, C. Burke. (1984). *Language stories and literacy lessons.* Portsmouth, NH: Heinemann.

Hebert, E. A. (1998, April). Lessons learned about student portfolios. *Phi Delta Kappan.* 79, 8, 583–85.

Hebert, E. (2001). *The power of portfolios*. San Francisco: Jossey-Bass

Holland, D. Lachicotte, W., Skinner, D., & Cain, C. (2001). *Agency and identity in cultural worlds*. Boston: Harvard University Press.

Jensen, E. J. (2007). *Introduction to brain-compatible learning*. Thousand Oaks, CA: Corwin Press.

Johnson, D. W., & Johnson, R. T. (1994). Preparing teachers to support inclusion: Preservice and inservice programs. In Thousand, J., Villa, A. and. Nevin, A. (Eds.), *Creativity and collaborative learning* pp. 42–50. Baltimore, MD: Brookes Press.

Johnson, D. W., & Johnson, R. T. (1996). The role of cooperative learning in assessing and communicating student learning. In T. R. Gusky, ed. *1996 ASCD yearbook: Communicating student learning* pp. 25–46. Alexandria, VA: Association for Supervision and Curriculum Development.

Johnson, D. W. & Johnson, R. T. (2007). *Cooperative learning and assessment*. Retrieved June 22, 2007, from http://www.co-operation.org/pages/assess.html.

Kingore, B. (2008). *Developing portfolios for authentic assessment, pre K–3: guiding potential in young learners*. Thousand Oaks,CA: Corwin Press.

Kohn, A. (1999, May). The dark side of standards. *Education Update*, 7.

Mele, A. R. (2005). *Motivation and human agency*. New York: Oxford University Press.

Mills-Court, K., & Amiran, R. (1991). Metacognition and the use of portfolios. In P. Belanoff, & M. Dickson (Eds.), *Portfolios: Process and product* (pp. 101–111). Portsmouth, NH: Baxton, & Court Publishers.

Missouri Department of Elementary and Secondary Education. (1993). *Show-me standards*. Jefferson City, MO: Missouri Department of Elementary and Secondary Education.

Montgomery, K., & Wiley, D. (2004). *Creating e-portfolios using PowerPoint*. Thousand Oaks, CA: Corwin Press.

National Middle School Association. (2006). Message from NMSA's Exective Director on Accountability and the Impact of High-Stakes Testing. www.nmsa.org/Advocacy/MessagesfromNMSA/HighStakesTesting

Niquida, D. (1993). The digital portfolio: A richer picture of student performance. In *The Exhibitions Collection*. Providence, RI: Coalition of Essential Schools, Brown University.

Paulson, E. L., P. R. Paulson, & C. A. Meyer. (1991, February). What makes a portfolio a portfolio? *Educational Leadership*, 60–63.

Popham, W. J. (1999). *Classroom assessment: What teachers need to know*, 2nd ed. Boston: Allyn, & Bacon.

Popham, J. (2003). *Trouble with testing*, National School Boards Association. Retrieved June 22, 2007, from http://www.nsba.org/site/site_index.asp.

Rolheiser, C., Bower, B., & Stevahn, L. (2000). *The portfolio organizer: Succeeding with portfolios in your classroom*. Alexandria, VA: Association for Supervision and Curriculum Development.

Saskatchewan Ministry of Education. (2007). *Sample Peer Assessment*. Retrieved June, 2007, from http://www.sasked.gov.sk.ca/docs/ela20/pg047.pdf.

Schlechty, P. (2005). *Creating great schools: Six critical systems at the heart of educational innovation*. San Francisco. Jossey-Bass

Silvers.P. (1994. April). Everyday signs of learning. *Primary Voices*, 20–29.

Smith, C. (1999). Assessing and reporting progress through student-led portfolio conferences. National Middle School Association, Westerville, OH. www.nmsa.org/Publications/WebExclusive/Portfolio/tabid/650/Default.aspx

Stefanakis, E. H. (2002). *Multiple intelligences and portfolios*. Portsmouth, NH: Heinemann.

Stefanakis, E.H. (2006). Failing our Students. *New York Times*. Retrieved April 22, 2007 from http://www.ccebos.org/nytimes.stefanakis.1.8.06.html.

Stiggins, R. J. (1994). *Student-centered classroom assessment*. New York: Merrill, MacMillan College Publishing.

Stiggins, R. J. (2002). Assessment crisis: The absence of assessment FOR learning. *Phi Delta Kappan*.

Sweet, D. (1993). Student portfolios: Classroom uses. *Education Research Consumer Guide*. Washington, DC: Office of Research, Office of Educational Research and Improvement of the U.S. Department of Education, Number 8.

Teachers College. 2006. When tests don't tell the full tale. Article 5618. Columbia University, New York. www.tc.columbia.edu/news/article.htm

Tomlinson, C., & Allan, S. 2000. *Leadership for differentiating schools and classrooms*. Alexandria, VA: Association for Supervision and Curriculum Development.

Tomlinson, C. A., & McTighe, J. (2006). *Integrating differentiated instruction and understanding by design*. Alexandria, VA: ASCD.

Tyler, R. (1969). *Basic principles of curriculum and instruction*. Chicago: University of Chicago Press.

Vavrus, L. 1990. August. Put portfolios to the test. *Instructor*. 48–53.

Wiggins, G. (1994). *Standards, not standardization* [Videotape]. Pleasantville, NY: Sunburst/Wings for Learning.

Wiggins, G., & McTighe, J. (1998). *Understanding by design*. Alexandria, VA: ASCD.

Wolf, D. (1989, April). Portfolio assessment: Sampling student work. *Educational Leadership*, 35–39.

Wortham, S. C. 2001. *Assessment in early childhood education* (3rd ed.). Upper Saddle River, NJ: Merrill Prentice Hall.

Additional Reading

American Educational Research Association. AERA: Position statement concerning high-stakes testing. Retrieved November 12, 2007, from http://www.aera.net/policyandprograms/?id=378 (Adopted, 2000).

Association for Supervision and Curriculum Development (2007). *Campaign for Whole Child Education.* www.wholechildeducation.org/about/

Belanoff, P., & Dickson, M. (1991). *Portfolios: Process and produc*t. Portsmouth, NH: Boyton, & Cook Publishers.

Bellanca, J., & Fogarty. R. (2003). *Blueprints for achievement in the cooperative classroom* (3rd ed.). Thousand Oaks, CA: Corwin Press.

Bellanca, J., Chapman, C., & Swartz, E. (1994). *Multiple assessments for multiple intelligences.* Thousand Oaks, CA: Corwin Press.

Black, P., & William, D. (1998, March). Assessment and classroom learning. *Assessment in Education,* 7–74.

Bower, B. E. (1994). *Assessment and evaluation. Mathematics in the transition years: A handbook for teachers of grade 9.* Durham, Ontario, Canada: Durham Board of Education.

Brady, G. (2000, May). The standards juggernaut. *Phi Delta Kappan,* 649–51.

Brooks, J., & M. Brooks. (1993). *In search of understanding: The case for constructivist classrooms.* Alexandria, VA: Association for Supervision and Curriculum Development.

Brown, G., & Irby, B. J. (1997). *The principal portfolio.* Thousand Oaks, CA: Corwin Press.

Brown, R. (1989, April). Testing and thoughtfulness. *Educational Leadership,* 31–33.

Brown, S. Rust, C., & Gibbs, G. (1994). Strategies for diversifying assessment in higher education. Oxford: Oxford Centre for Staff Development

Burke, K. 2004. *How to assess authentic learning* (4th ed.). Thousand Oaks, CA: Corwin Press.

Burke, K. 2005. *What to do with the kid who . . .* (2nd ed.). Thousand Oaks, CA: Corwin Press.

Catalyst. (2007). *Designing a portfolio.* Seattle: University of Washington. catalyst. washington.edu/help/planning/portfolio_design.html

Costa, A. L. (1993). Thinking: How do we know students are getting better at it? In K. A. Burke, ed. *Authentic assessment: A collection* (pp. 213–220). Thousand Oaks, CA: Corwin Press.

Costa, A. L., & Kallick, B. (2006). Describing 16 habits of mind. www.habits-of-mind.net/pdf/16HOM2.pdf

Costa, A. L., Bellanca, J., & Fogarty, R. (1992). *If minds matter: A foreword to the future,* Vol. I. Thousand Oaks, CA: Corwin Press.

Council for Exceptional Children. (2005). New CEC policy on high stakes assessment. www.cec.sped.org/Content/NavigationMenu/Publications2/CECToday/New_CEC_Policy_on_High_Stakes_Assessment.htm

Crafton, L. (1994, April). Reflections. *Primary Voices*, 39–42.

Danielson, C. (1996). *Enhancing professional practice: A framework for teaching*. Alexandria, VA: Association for Supervision and Curriculum Development.

Eisner, G. W. (1993, February). Why standards may not improve schools. *Educational Leadership*, 22–23.

European Institute for E-Learning. (2006). Why do we need an e-portfolio? Champiost, France: EIfEL (European Institute for E-Learning). www.eife-l.org/publications/e-portfolio/

Flavell, J. H., Fredenchs, A. G., & Hoyt, J. D. (1970). Development changes in memorization processes. *Cognitive Psychology*, *1*, 4, 324–40.

Fogarty, R. (1991). *The mindful school: How to integrate the curricula*. Thousand Oaks, CA: Corwin Press.

Fogarty, R. (1994). *The mindful school: How to teach for metacognitive reflection*. Thousand Oaks, CA: Corwin Press.

Fogarty, R., & Bellanca, J. (1989). *Patterns for thinking: Patterns for transfer*. Thousand Oaks, CA: Corwin Press.

Frazier, D., & Paulson, E. (1992, May). How portfolios motivate reluctant writers. *Educational Leadership*, 62–65.

Fusco, E., & Fountain, A. (1992). Reflective teacher, reflective learner. In A. L. Costa, J. Bellanca, & R. Fogarty (Eds.), *If minds matter: A foreword to the future*, Vol. I (pp. 239–255). Thousand Oaks, CA: Corwin Press.

Glazer, S. M. (1993, December). How do I grade without grades? *Teaching K–8*, 104–106.

Goodman, K., Bird, L. B., & Goodman, Y. M. (Eds.), (1992). *The whole language supplement on authentic assessment: Evaluating ourselves*. New York: SRA Macmillan/McGraw-Hill.

Gronlund, N. E. (1998). *Assessment of student achievement* (6th ed.). Boston: Allyn & Bacon.

Hamm, M., & Adams, D. (1991, May). Portfolio: It's not just for artists anymore. *The Science Teacher*, 18–21.

Hebert, E. A. (1992, May). Portfolios invite reflection—from students and staff. *Educational Leadership*, 61.

International Reading Association. (2006). Call for proposals in technology, communication, and literacy committee. Newark, DE: IRA.

Johnson, D. W., & Johnson, R. T. (2006). Cooperative learning and assessment. The Cooperative Learning Center. www.co-operation.org/pages/assess.html

Nitko, A. J. (2001). *Educational assessment of students*, 3rd ed. Upper Saddle River, NJ: Prentice Hall.

Peter, L. J. (1977). *Peter's quotations: Ideas for our time*. New York: Bantam.

Popham, W. (2003). *Trouble with Testing*. National School Boards Association. Arlington, VA.

Popham, W. J. (2000). *Testing! Testing! What every parent should know about school tests*. Boston: Allyn, & Bacon.

Popham, W. J. (2003). *What every teacher should know about educational assessment*. Boston: Pearson Education.

Rolhesier, C., ed. (1996). *Self-evaluation . . . Helping students get better at it!* Ajax, Ontario, Canada: VisuTron X.

Schlechty, P. (2002). *Working on the work*. San Francisco: Jossey Bass.

Schlechty, P. (2004). No child left behind: Noble sentiment and poor design. Occasional Paper. Louisville, KY: Schlechty Center for Leadership and School Reform.

Schoenfeld, A. H. (1987). What's all the fuss about metacognition? In A. H. Schoenfeld, ed. Cognitive science and mathematics education (everyday signs of learning). *Primary Voices*, 20–29.

Stefanakis, E. H. (2006, January 8). Failing our students. *New York Times*.

Tomlinson, C. A. (1999). *The differentiated classroom: Responding to the needs of all learners.* Alexandria, VA: Association for Supervision and Curriculum Development.

Wiggins, G. (1993). *Assessing student performance: Exploring the purpose and limits of testing.* San Francisco: Jossey-Bass.

Index

CORWIN PRESS

The Corwin Press logo—a raven striding across an open book—represents the union of courage and learning. Corwin Press is committed to improving education for all learners by publishing books and other professional development resources for those serving the field of PreK–12 education. By providing practical, hands-on materials, Corwin Press continues to carry out the promise of its motto: **"Helping Educators Do Their Work Better."**